HOLT McDOUGAL

LARSON
ALGEBRA 1

COMMON CORE **State Standards**
Curriculum Companion

Student Edition

Ron Larson

Laurie Boswell

Timothy D. Kanold

Lee Stiff

HOLT McDOUGAL

HOUGHTON MIFFLIN HARCOURT

COMMON CORE

Larson Algebra 1
Common Core State Standards
Curriculum Companion
Student Edition

Contents

Lesson 1.5A   Use Precision and Measurement **CC1**

Extension 3.1   Use Real and Rational Numbers **CC8**

Extension 3.4   Apply Properties of Equality **CC11**

Graphing Calculator Activity 4.7
Solving Linear Equations by Graphing Each Side **CC13**

Extension 5.7   Assess the Fit of a Model **CC15**

Graphing Calculator Activity 7.4
Multiply and Then Add Equations **CC18**

Lesson 10.7A   Solve Systems with Quadratic Equations **CC21**

Lesson 10.8A   Model Relationships **CC28**

Graphing Calculator Activity 10.8A
Average Rate of Change **CC35**

Investigating Algebra Activity 13.5
Investigating Samples **CC36**

Lesson 13.6A   Analyze Data **CC37**

Investigating Algebra Activity 13.7   Investigate Dot Plots **CC42**

Extension 13.8   Analyze Data **CC44**

1.5A Use Precision and Measurement

Before	You measured using a ruler and protractor.
Now	You will compare measurements for precision.
Why?	So you can determine which measurement is more precise, as in Ex. 31.

Key Vocabulary
• precision
• significant digits

You ask two friends for the time. Noah says that it is about 2:30. Mia says it is 2:28 and 19 seconds. Mia gives a more *precise* measurement of the time.

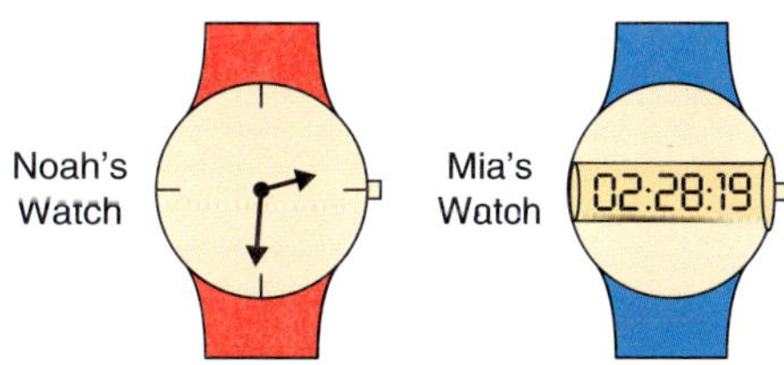

PRECISION Precision is the level of detail that an instrument can measure. Mia's watch is more precise than Noah's watch because it gives the time to the nearest second. In a similar way, a ruler marked in millimeters is more precise than a ruler marked only in centimeters, since a millimeter is a smaller unit than a centimeter.

EXAMPLE 1 Compare precision of measurements

Choose the more precise measurement.

a. 7 cm; 7.3 cm   **b.** 5 yd; 16 ft   **c.** 1 pint; 16 ounces

Solution

AVOID ERRORS
Remember that the smaller number is not always the more precise measurement. Always examine the units of measure.

a. The units are the same. Because tenths are smaller than ones, 7.3 centimeters is more precise than 7 centimeters.

b. The units are different. Because a foot is a smaller unit of measure than a yard, 16 feet is a more precise unit of measure.

c. The units are different. Because an ounce is a smaller unit of measure than a pint, 16 ounces is a more precise measurement even though 1 pint is equal to 16 ounces.

✓ **GUIDED PRACTICE** for Example 1

Choose the more precise measurement.

1. 21.13 oz; 21.4 oz

2. $14\frac{1}{2}$ in.; $2\frac{5}{8}$ in.

3. 14 mm; 2 cm

4. 2.5 hr; 90 min

SIGNIFICANT DIGITS To the nearest centimeter, the diameter of a United States quarter is 2 centimeters. Measured to the nearest millimeter, the diameter of the quarter is 24 millimeters. The measurement 24 millimeters is more precise because it is given using a smaller unit of length.

In the two coin measurements, notice that the numerical value 24 has more digits than the value 2. You can use the number of significant digits to describe the precision of a measurement. **Significant digits** are the digits in a measurement that carry meaning contributing to the precision of the measurement.

KEY CONCEPT *For Your Notebook*

Determining Significant Digits

Rule	Example	Significant digits	Number of significant digits
All nonzero digits	281.39	**281.39**	5
Zeros that are to the right of both the last nonzero digit and the decimal point	0.0070	0.00**70**	2
Zeros between significant digits	500.7	**500.7**	4

Zeros at the end of a whole number are usually assumed to be nonsignificant. For example, 220 centimeters has 2 significant digits, while 202 centimeters has 3 significant digits.

EXAMPLE 2 Identify significant digits

Determine the number of significant digits in each measurement.

   a. 290.01 g   **b.** 0.8500 km   **c.** 4000 mi

Solution

a. The digits 2, 9, and 1 are nonzero digits, so they are significant digits. The zeros are between significant digits, so they are also significant digits.

There are 5 significant digits: **290.01**.

b. The digits 8 and 5 are nonzero digits, so they are significant digits. The two zeros to the right of the last nonzero digit are also to the right of the decimal point, so they are significant digits.

There are 4 significant digits: 0.**8500**.

c. The digit 4 is a nonzero digit, so it is a significant digit. The zeros at the end of a whole number are not significant.

There is 1 significant digit: **4**000.

AVOID ERRORS
Remember that not all zeros are significant. Be careful when deciding whether a zero in a number is significant or not.

SIGNIFICANT DIGITS IN CALCULATIONS When you perform calculations involving measurements, the number of significant digits that you write in your result depends on the number of significant digits in the given measurements.

<table>
<tr><td colspan="3">KEY CONCEPT   For Your Notebook</td></tr>
<tr><td colspan="3">Determining Significant Digits in Calculations</td></tr>
<tr><th>Operations</th><th>Rule</th><th>Example</th></tr>
<tr><td>Addition and Subtraction</td><td>Round the sum or difference to the same place as the last significant digit of the least precise measurement.</td><td>3.24 ← hundredths
+ 7.3   ← tenths
10.54 ← tenths</td></tr>
<tr><td>Multiplication and Division</td><td>The product or quotient must have the same number of significant digits as the least precise measurement.</td><td>40 ← 1 sig digit
× 31 ← 2 sig digits
1240 ← exact answer
1000 ← 1 sig digit</td></tr>
</table>

Zeros at the end of a whole number are usually assumed to be nonsignificant. For example, 220 centimeters has 2 significant digits, while 202 centimeters has 3 significant digits.

EXAMPLE 3   Calculating with significant digits

Perform the indicated operation. Write the answer with the correct number of significant digits.

  a. 45.1 cm + 19.45 cm   **b.** 6.4 ft $\times$ 2.15 ft

Solution

  a. 45.1 cm + 19.45 cm = 64.55 cm

     The least precise measurement is 45.1 centimeters. Its last significant digit is in the tenths place. Round the sum to the nearest tenth.

     The correct sum is 64.6 centimeters.

  b. 6.4 ft $\times$ 2.15 ft = 13.76 ft^2

     The least precise measurement is 6.4 feet. It has two significant digits. Round the product to two significant digits.

     The correct product is 14 square feet.

✓ **GUIDED PRACTICE**   for Examples 2 and 3

Determine the number of significant digits in each measurement.

  5. 800.20 ft   **6.** 0.005 cm   **7.** 36,900 mi

Perform the indicated operation. Write the answer with the correct number of significant digits.

  8. 27.23 m − 12.7 m   **9.** 45.16 yd^2 ÷ 4.25 yd

1.5A EXERCISES

SKILL PRACTICE

1. **VOCABULARY** Copy and complete: The level of detail that an instrument can measure is known as its ? .

2. ★ **WRITING** Which number, 0.023 or 301, has the fewer significant digits? Explain.

EXAMPLE 1
on p. CC1
for Exs. 3–10

COMPARING PRECISION Choose the more precise measurement.

○ **3.** 14.2 gal; 7 gal

4. 0.02 mm; 0.1 mm

5. 90 ft; 71 in.

6. 57.65 lb; 34.9 lb

7. 14.1 m; 29.3 cm

8. 36 yd; 17.2 yd

ERROR ANALYSIS Describe and correct the error in the statement.

9. Heidi told her friend Mike that 1.5 hours is a more precise measurement of time than 85 minutes.

10. Eric's new fishing rod was advertised as being 4 feet long. He measured it to be 47 inches long. Eric's friend says that 4 feet is the more precise measurement.

EXAMPLE 2
on p. CC2
for Exs. 11–20

IDENTIFYING SIGNIFICANT DIGITS Determine the number of significant digits in the measurement.

○ **11.** 312.5 cm

12. 100 hr

13. 0.030 gal

14. 16.007 lb

15. 1020 mm

16. 0.0025 sec

17. 38.0 m

18. 8.375 ft

19. 205.7140 mi

20. ★ **MULTIPLE CHOICE** The measurement 0.007 grams contains how many significant digits?

Ⓐ 1 Ⓑ 2 Ⓒ 3 Ⓓ 4

EXAMPLE 3
on p. CC3
for Exs. 21–30

CALCULATING WITH SIGNIFICANT DIGITS Perform the indicated operation. Write the answer with the correct number of significant digits.

○ **21.** 97.2 m − 16.04 m

22. 8 ft × 11.2 ft

23. 257.64 oz ÷ 2.4 oz

24. 0.043 yd + 0.22 yd

25. 6.42 mm × 7.51 mm

26. 2.8 mi + 3.56 mi

27. 245 kg − 18.32 kg

28. 9.05 cm² ÷ 18 cm

29. ★ **WRITING** Describe how to find the number of significant digits to give for the area of a rectangle with side lengths 8.2 meters and 20 meters.

30. ★ **MULTIPLE CHOICE** The quotient 97.3 hr ÷ 5.5 hr contains how many significant digits?

Ⓐ 4 Ⓑ 3 Ⓒ 2 Ⓓ 1

CHALLENGE Perform the indicated operation. Write the answer with the correct number of significant digits.

31. 0.40 ft × 2.25 ft

32. 23.175 km² ÷ 10.30 km

EXAMPLE 1
on p. CC1
for Exs. 33–36

33. **COINS** According to the United States Mint, a one-dollar coin has a mass of 8.1 grams. Justine finds the mass of a one-dollar coin and reports a mass of 8.05 grams. Steven finds that the mass of his one-dollar coin is 8.2 grams. Whose measurement is more precise?

COMPARING MEASUREMENTS For Exercises 34–36, three students are asked to measure a piece of string that has a length of exactly 15.2 centimeters. Their measurements are shown in the table.

Student	Measurement
Alex	15.35 cm
Chandra	14.9 cm
Luis	154 mm

34. Which student made the most precise measurement?

35. Which student made the least precise measurement?

36. Which student's answer is closest to the actual length of the string?

EXAMPLES
2 and 3
on pp. CC2–3
for Exs. 37–49

37. ★ **SHORT RESPONSE** Brian drives 426 miles and uses 19.3 gallons of gas for the trip. Brian's calculator shows that $\frac{426}{19.3} \approx 22.07253886$, so he states that his car gets 22.07253886 miles per gallon. Do you agree with Brian's statement? *Explain* your answer?

38. **REFLECTING POOL** The Reflecting Pool is a rectangular body of water in front of the Lincoln Memorial in Washington, D.C. A surveyor determines that the length of the pool to the nearest foot is 2029 feet and the width of the pool to the nearest foot is 167 feet.

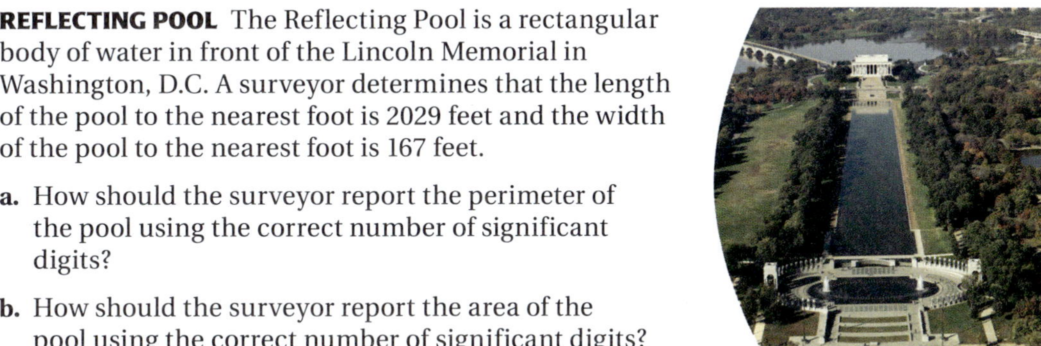

  a. How should the surveyor report the perimeter of the pool using the correct number of significant digits?

  b. How should the surveyor report the area of the pool using the correct number of significant digits?

39. **HEALTH** When Kyle went for his annual physical the nurse weighed him and told him he weighed 118.5 pounds. After seeing the doctor, Kyle was sent for some tests where he was weighed again. This time he was told he weighed 119 pounds. Which of the two measurements is more precise? *Explain* your answer.

40. **GARDENING** A student measures the length of a rectangular garden plot to the nearest tenth of a meter and finds that the length is 6.4 meters. Another student measures the width of the plot to the nearest meter and finds that the width is 2 meters. Using the correct number of significant digits, what are the perimeter and area of the plot?

41. **CHARITY RUN** Nicole and Renee are participating in a charity run to raise money for their school's library. Both girls have sponsors who will pay them $1 for each mile they collectively run. If Nicole ran 7.2 miles and Renee ran 6.03 miles, how should they report their cumulative miles to their sponsors using the correct number of significant digits?

★ **OPEN-ENDED** In Exercises 42–46, give an example of the described measurement.

42. A 5-digit distance in miles that has 3 significant digits

43. A measurement greater than 1000 centimeters that has 2 significant digits

44. A measurement less than 1 millimeter that has 4 significant digits

45. A 4-digit area that has 3 significant digits and 2 digits that are zeros

46. A weight less than 10 pounds that has 5 significant digits

47. **POSTERS** The area of a rectangular poster is 852 square inches. The length of the poster is 36 inches. Using the correct number of significant digits, what is the width of the poster?

48. **SCIENCE** Tanya and Edmond are lab partners in science class. They each measure the volume of a beaker of a solution. Tanya found the volume to be 2.25 liters, while Edmond reported the volume as 2300 milliliters. Who gave the more precise measurement? *Explain* your answer.

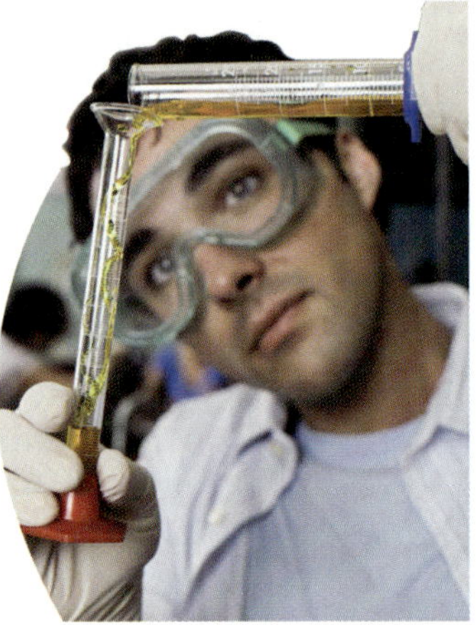

49. **REALTORS** When a realtor first lists a home for sale, it is very important to calculate the living area of the home. Carrie measured the length and width of a house she is about to list and found that it measured 52.5 feet long by 35 feet wide. Using the correct number of significant digits, how should Carrie report the area of the house?

50. **CHALLENGE** A student measures the length of a cube and records the length as 3.5 centimeters. Using the correct number of significant digits, how should the student report the volume of the cube?

51. **CHALLENGE** Suppose the average 12-ounce aluminum drink can weighs approximately 13.6 grams and the liquid inside weighs approximately 453.59 grams. Using the correct number of significant digits, how much do the 24 drink cans in a carton weigh?

MIXED REVIEW

PREVIEW
Prepare for Lesson 1.6 in Exs. 52–56.

Evaluate the expression. *(Lesson 1.2)*

52. $4^2 + 8 \div 2$ 53. $42 - 1 \times 5$ 54. $40 - [2^3 - 1]$

Evaluate the expression when $x = -2$. *(Lesson 1.2)*

55. $x^2 + 3$ 56. $-5x - 5$ 57. $-4(x - 2)$

58. **AREA** A football field is 50 yards wide and 100 yards long. What is the area of the field? *(Lesson 1.5)*

Mastering *the* Standards

for Mathematical Practice

The topics described in the Standards for Mathematical Content will vary from year to year. However, the *way* in which you learn, study, and think about mathematics will not. The Standards for Mathematical Practice describe skills that you will use in all of your math courses.

Mathematical Practices

1. *Make sense of problems and persevere in solving them.*
2. *Reason abstractly and quantitatively.*
3. *Construct viable arguments and critique the reasoning of others.*
4. *Model with mathematics.*
5. *Use appropriate tools strategically.*
6. *Attend to precision.*
7. *Look for and make use of structure.*
8. *Look for and express regularity in repeated reasoning.*

① Make sense of problems and persevere in solving them.

Mathematically proficient students start by explaining to themselves the meaning of a problem... They analyze givens, constraints, relationships, and goals. They make conjectures about the form... of the solution and plan a solution pathway...

In your book

Verbal Models and the **Problem Solving Plan** help you translate the information in a problem into a model and then analyze your solution.

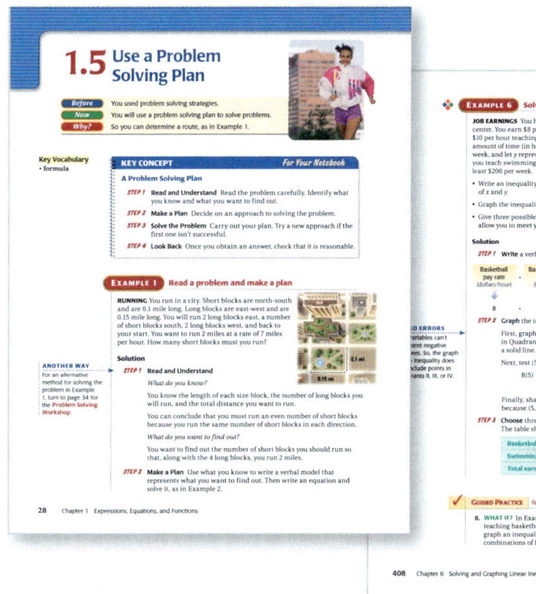

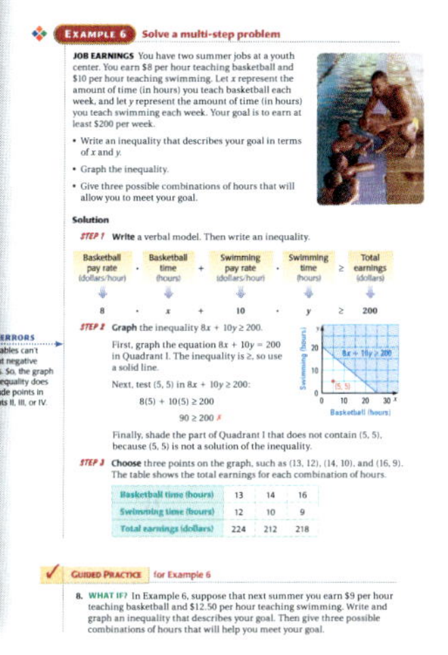

Use Real and Rational Numbers

GOAL Identify whether sets of rational and irrational numbers are closed under operations.

Key Vocabulary
• closure

RATIONAL AND IRRATIONAL NUMBERS Recall that a *rational number* is a number $\frac{a}{b}$ where a and b are integers with $b \neq 0$. An *irrational number* is any number that cannot be written as a quotient of two integers.

EXAMPLE 1 Sums of rational numbers

Prove that the sum of two rational numbers is rational.

Solution

Let x and y be two rational numbers.

By the definition of rational numbers, x can be written as $\frac{a}{b}$ and y can be written as $\frac{c}{d}$ where a, b, c, and d are integers with $b \neq 0$ and $d \neq 0$.

$$x + y = \frac{a}{b} + \frac{c}{d} \qquad \text{Add } x \text{ and } y.$$

$$x + y = \frac{ad + bc}{bd} \qquad \text{Rewrite } \frac{a}{b} + \frac{c}{d} \text{ using a common denominator.}$$

Because the sum or product of two integers will always be integers, the expressions $ad + bc$ and bd are both integers.

Therefore, the sum $x + y$ is equal to the ratio of two integers. So by definition, this sum is a rational number.

CLOSURE As you saw in Example 1, the sum of two rational numbers is rational. The set of rational numbers has *closure* or is *closed* under multiplication.

KEY CONCEPT *For Your Notebook*

Closure

A set has **closure** or is closed under a given operation if the number that results from performing the operation on any two numbers in the set is also in the set.

Example: The sum of any two rational numbers is a rational number. The set of rationals is closed under addition.

$$\frac{1}{2} + \frac{1}{3} = \frac{5}{6} \qquad\qquad \frac{1}{2} + \frac{3}{2} = 2$$

Non-example: The quotient of two integers is not necessarily an integer. The set of integers is not closed under division.

$$6 \div 2 = 3 \qquad\qquad -6 \div 5 = -\frac{6}{5}$$

> ## EXAMPLE 2 Sum of a rational and an irrational number
>
> **Solve the equation $x - 3 = \sqrt{2}$. Is the solution _rational_ or _irrational_?**
>
> ### Solution
>
> $$x - 3 = \sqrt{2} \qquad \text{Write original equation.}$$
>
> $$x - 3 + 3 = \sqrt{2} + 3 \qquad \text{Add 3 to both sides.}$$
>
> $$x = \sqrt{2} + 3 \qquad \text{Simplify.}$$
>
> ▶ The solution is _irrational_.

SUMS OF IRRATIONAL NUMBERS Example 2 shows a single case where the sum of a rational number and an irrational number is irrational. To prove that this is always true, you must first assume that such a sum is rational. This results in a contradiction which proves that the assumption must be false.

Let a be rational and b be irrational. Let c be the sum of a and b, and assume that c is rational.

$$a + b = c \qquad \text{Assume } c \text{ is rational.}$$

$$b = c - a \qquad \text{Subtract } a \text{ from each side.}$$

By Example 1, you know that $c - a$ is rational. But a rational number cannot be equal to an irrational number, so this is a contradiction. Therefore the sum of a rational number and an irrational number must be irrational.

PRACTICE

1. Use Example 1 as a model to prove that the product of two rational numbers is rational.

2. Copy and complete: Prove that the product of a nonzero rational number and an irrational number is irrational.

Let x be a rational number and y be an __?__ number. By definition, $x = \dfrac{a}{b}$, where a and b are __?__ with $b \neq 0$. Now assume that the product xy is a __?__ number. Therefore xy can be written as the quotient of integers c and d with $d \neq 0$.

__?__	The product xy can be written as $\dfrac{c}{d}$.
__?__	Substitute $\dfrac{a}{b}$ for x.
__?__	Multiply both sides by __?__ .
__?__	Simplify.

By definition, __?__ is a rational number which means that y must be rational. But y is an irrational number, meaning the assumption that __?__ is rational must be false. Therefore, __?__ .

---

3. Use an indirect proof like the one following Example 2 to prove that the sum of a rational number and an irrational number is irrational.

Mastering the Standards

for Mathematical Practice

The topics described in the Standards for Mathematical Content will vary from year to year. However, the *way* in which you learn, study, and think about mathematics will not. The Standards for Mathematical Practice describe skills that you will use in all of your math courses.

Mathematical Practices

1. *Make sense of problems and persevere in solving them.*
2. *Reason abstractly and quantitatively.*
3. *Construct viable arguments and critique the reasoning of others.*
4. *Model with mathematics.*
5. *Use appropriate tools strategically.*
6. *Attend to precision.*
7. *Look for and make use of structure.*
8. *Look for and express regularity in repeated reasoning.*

4 Model with mathematics.

Mathematically proficient students can apply... mathematics... to... problems... in everyday life, society, and the workplace...

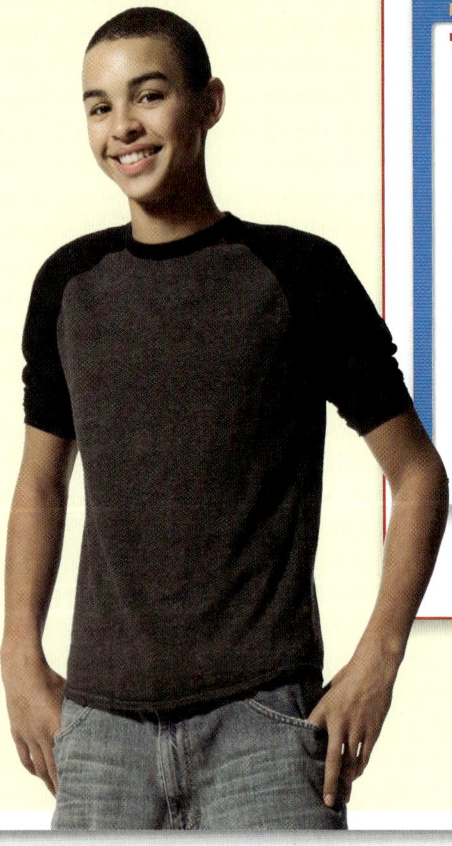

In your book

Application exercises and **Mixed Reviews of Problem Solving** apply mathematics to other disciplines and in real-world scenarios.

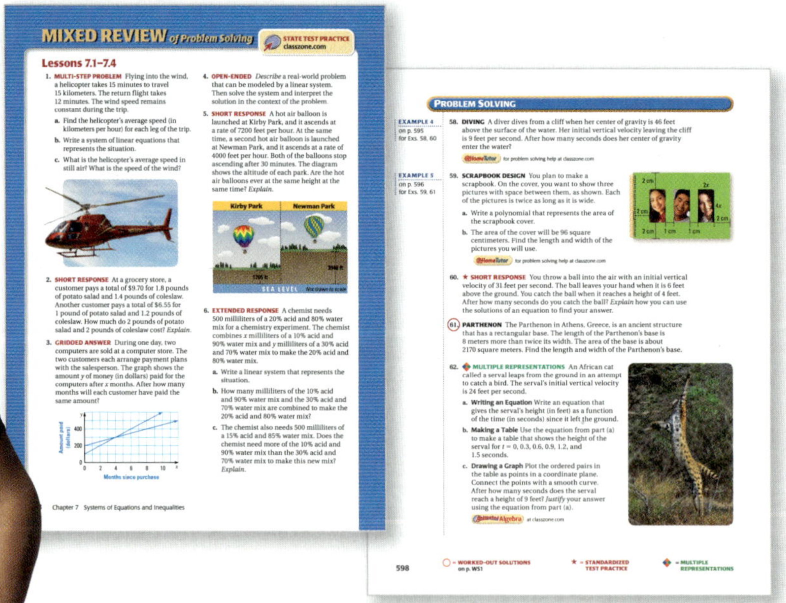

MIXED REVIEW of Problem Solving

STATE TEST PRACTICE classzone.com

Lessons 7.1–7.4

1. **MULTI-STEP PROBLEM** Flying into the wind, a helicopter takes 15 minutes to travel 15 kilometers. The return flight takes 12 minutes. The wind speed remains constant during the trip.
   a. Find the helicopter's average speed (in kilometers per hour) for each leg of the trip.
   b. Write a system of linear equations that represents the situation.
   c. What is the helicopter's average speed in still air? What is the speed of the wind?
2. **SHORT RESPONSE** At a grocery store, a customer pays a total of \$9.70 for 1.8 pounds of potato salad and 1.4 pounds of coleslaw. Another customer pays a total of \$6.55 for 1 pound of potato salad and 1.2 pounds of coleslaw. How much do 2 pounds of potato salad and 2 pounds of coleslaw cost? *Explain.*
3. **GRIDDED ANSWER** During one day, two computers are sold at a computer store. The two customers each arrange payment plans with the salesperson. The graph shows the amount y of money (in dollars) paid for the computers after x months. After how many months will each customer have paid the same amount?
4. **OPEN-ENDED** *Describe* a real-world problem that can be modeled by a linear system. Then solve the system and interpret the solution in the context of the problem.
5. **SHORT RESPONSE** A hot air balloon is launched at Kirby Park, and it ascends at a rate of 7200 feet per hour. At the same time, a second hot air balloon is launched at Newman Park, and it ascends at a rate of 4000 feet per hour. Both of the balloons stop ascending after 30 minutes. The diagram shows the altitude of each park. Are the hot air balloons ever at the same height at the same time? *Explain.*
6. **EXTENDED RESPONSE** A chemist needs 500 milliliters of a 20% acid and 80% water mix for a chemistry experiment. The chemist combines x milliliters of a 10% acid and 90% water mix and y milliliters of a 30% acid and 70% water mix to make the 20% acid and 80% water mix.
   a. Write a linear system that represents the situation.
   b. How many milliliters of the 10% acid and 90% water mix and the 30% acid and 70% water mix are combined to make the 20% acid and 80% water mix?
   c. The chemist also needs 500 milliliters of a 15% acid and 85% water mix. Does the chemist need more of the 10% acid and 90% water mix than the 30% acid and 70% water mix to make this new mix? *Explain.*

Chapter 7 Systems of Equations and Inequalities

PROBLEM SOLVING

EXAMPLE 4 on p. 595 for Exs. 58, 60

58. **DIVING** A diver dives from a cliff when her center of gravity is 46 feet above the surface of the water. Her initial vertical velocity leaving the cliff is 9 feet per second. After how many seconds does her center of gravity enter the water?

@HomeTutor for problem solving help at classzone.com

EXAMPLE 5 on p. 596 for Exs. 59, 61

59. **SCRAPBOOK DESIGN** You plan to make a scrapbook. On the cover, you want to show three pictures with space between them, as shown. Each of the pictures is twice as long as it is wide.
   a. Write a polynomial that represents the area of the scrapbook cover.
   b. The area of the cover will be 96 square centimeters. Find the length and width of the pictures you will use.

@HomeTutor for problem solving help at classzone.com

60. ★ **SHORT RESPONSE** You throw a ball into the air with an initial vertical velocity of 31 feet per second. The ball leaves your hand when it is 6 feet above the ground. You catch the ball when it reaches a height of 4 feet. After how many seconds do you catch the ball? *Explain* how you can use the solutions of an equation to find your answer.
61. **PARTHENON** The Parthenon in Athens, Greece, is an ancient structure that has a rectangular base. The length of the Parthenon's base is 8 meters more than twice its width. The area of the base is about 2170 square meters. Find the length and width of the Parthenon's base.
62. ◆ **MULTIPLE REPRESENTATIONS** An African cat called a serval leaps from the ground in an attempt to catch a bird. The serval's initial vertical velocity is 24 feet per second.
   a. **Writing an Equation** Write an equation that gives the serval's height (in feet) as a function of the time (in seconds) since it left the ground.
   b. **Making a Table** Use the equation from part (a) to make a table that shows the height of the serval for $t = 0, 0.3, 0.6, 0.9, 1.2,$ and 1.5 seconds.
   c. **Drawing a Graph** Plot the ordered pairs in the table as points in a coordinate plane. Connect the points with a smooth curve. After how many seconds does the serval reach a height of 9 feet? *Justify* your answer using the equation from part (a).

Animated Algebra at classzone.com

598 ○ = WORKED-OUT SOLUTIONS on p. WS1 ★ = STANDARDIZED TEST PRACTICE ◆ = MULTIPLE REPRESENTATIONS

Apply Properties of Equality

Use after Lesson 3.4

GOAL Use algebraic properties to help solve equations.

Key Vocabulary
• equation
• solve an equation

When you *solve an equation*, you use properties of real numbers. In particular you use the *algebraic properties of equality* and the *distributive property*.

KEY CONCEPT
For Your Notebook

Algebraic Properties of Equality

Let a, b, and c be real numbers.

Addition Property	If $a = b$, then $a + c = b + c$.
Subtraction Property	If $a = b$, then $a - c = b - c$.
Multiplication Property	If $a = b$, then $ac = bc$.
Division Property	If $a = b$ and $c \neq 0$, then $\frac{a}{c} = \frac{b}{c}$.
Substitution Property	If $a = b$, then a can be substituted for b in any equation or expression.

EXAMPLE 1 Write reasons for each step

Solve $4x + 7 = -2x - 5$. Write reasons for each step.

Solution

Equation	Explanation	Reason
$4x + 7 = -2x - 5$	Write original equation.	Given
$4x + 7 + 2x = -2x - 5 + 2x$	Add $2x$ to each side.	Addition Property of Equality
$6x + 7 = -5$	Combine like terms.	Simplify.
$6x + 7 - 7 = -5 - 7$	Subtract 7 from each side.	Subtraction Property of Equality
$6x = -12$	Combine like terms.	Simplify.
$x = -2$	Divide each side by 6.	Division Property of Equality

▶ The value of x is -2.

 **GUIDED PRACTICE** for Example 1

Solve the equation. Write a reason for each step.

1. $5x - 7 = 8$

2. $13 - 2x = x + 25$

EXAMPLE 2 **Use the Distributive Property**

Solve $7(5 - x) = 14$. Write reasons for each step.

Solution

Equation	Explanation	Reason
$7(5 - x) = 14$	Write original equation.	Given
$35 - 7x = 14$	Multiply.	Distributive Property
$-7x = -21$	Subtract 35 from each side.	Subtraction Property of Equality
$x = 3$	Divide each side by -7.	Division Property of Equality

▶ The value of x is 3.

PRACTICE

Copy the logical argument. Write a reason for each step.

1. $3x - 12 = 7x + 8$ Given
    $-4x - 12 = 8$?
    $-4x = 20$?
    $x = -5$?

2. $5(x - 1) = 4x + 3$ Given
    $5x - 5 = 4x + 3$?
    $x - 5 = 3$?
    $x = 8$?

For Exercises 3–14, solve the equation. Write a reason for each step.

3. $5x - 10 = -40$
4. $4x + 9 = 16 - 3x$
5. $5 - x = 17$
6. $2x - 3 = x - 5$
7. $19 - 2x = -17$
8. $-3x = -5x + 12$
9. $5(3x - 20) = -10$
10. $3(2x + 11) = 9$
11. $2(-x - 5) = 12$
12. $4(5x - 9) = -2(x + 7)$
13. $13 - x = -2(x + 3)$
14. $3(7x - 9) - 19x = -15$

15. **ERROR ANALYSIS** Describe and correct the error in solving for x.

$7x = x + 24$ Given	
$8x = 24$ Addition Property of Equality	
$x = 3$ Division Property of Equality	

16. **DEBATE** Mrs. Sinclair divided her 30 history students into 6 debate teams, with each team consisting of a secretary to take notes during the debates and x debaters. The solution of the equation $6(x + 1) = 30$ represents the number of debaters on each team. Solve the equation and write a reason for each step.

4.7 Solving Linear Equations by Graphing Each Side

QUESTION How can a graphing calculator be used to solve a linear equation?

You can solve a linear equation in one variable by graphing each side of the equation and finding the point of intersection. The *x*-value of the intersection is the solution of the equation.

EXAMPLE 1 Solve a linear equation

Solve the linear equation $\frac{4}{5}x + 8 = 20$ using a graphing calculator.

STEP 1 *Create two equations*

Write two functions by setting each side of the equation equal to *y*.

$$\frac{4}{5}x + 8 = 20$$

$$y = \frac{4}{5}x + 8 \text{ and } y = 20$$

STEP 2 *Enter equations*

Enter the equations from Step 1 as Y_1 and Y_2.

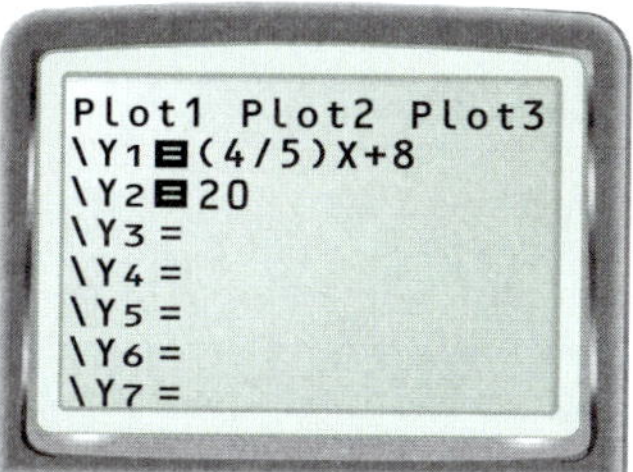

STEP 3 *Graph the equations*

Choose a viewing window that allows you to see the intersection.

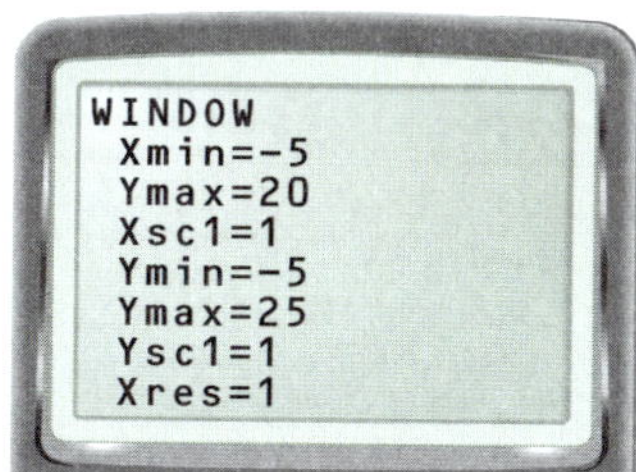

STEP 4 *Find the point of intersection*

Use the *Intersect* feature on the graphing calculator to find the point of intersection. The graphs intersect at (15, 20).

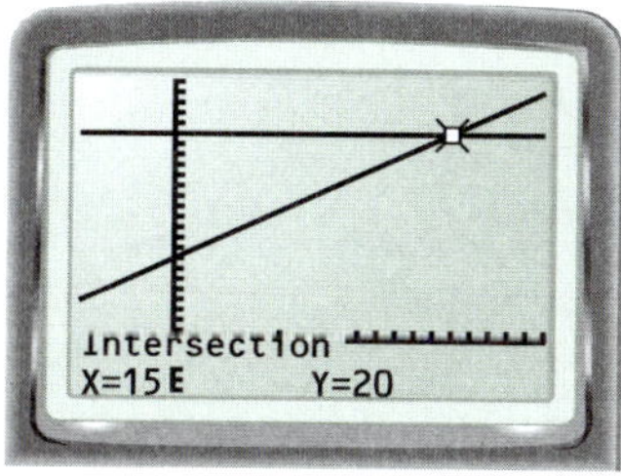

STEP 5 *Check the solution*

The *x*-value of the point of intersection, 15, is the solution of the equation. Check by substituting 15 for *x* in the original equation.

Check:

$$\frac{4}{5}x + 8 \stackrel{?}{=} 20$$

$$\frac{4}{5}(15) + 8 \stackrel{?}{=} 20$$

$$12 + 8 \stackrel{?}{=} 20$$

$$20 = 20 \checkmark$$

You can use this method to find a solution for any type of equation in one variable. You can also use this method to check a solution that you found algebraically.

PRACTICE 1

Solve the equation using a graphing calculator.

1. $6x - 5 = 19$

2. $3 = 2x + 5$

3. $-3q + 4 = 13$

4. $3 + \frac{8}{7}x = -1$

5. $7 - \frac{5}{3}c = 17$

6. $\frac{1}{3}x + \frac{2}{5}x = 22$

EXAMPLE 2 Solve a linear equation

Solve the linear equation $2t - 1 = -3t + 9$ using a graphing calculator.

STEP 1 Create two equations

Set each side of the equation equal to y and change t to x.

$$y = 2x - 1 \qquad y = -3x + 9$$

STEP 2 Enter equations

STEP 3 Graph the equations

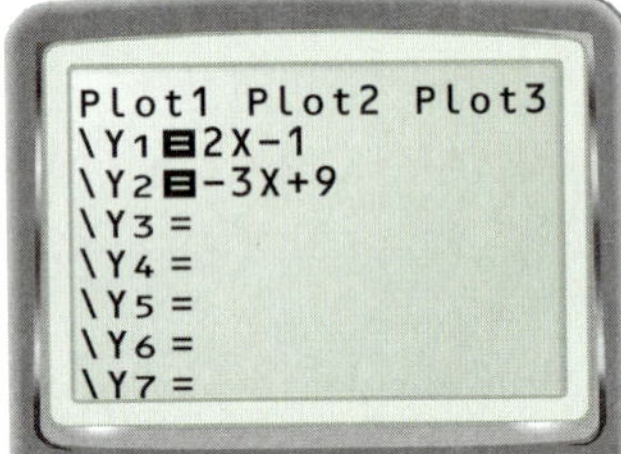

STEP 4 Find the point of intersection

Use the *Intersect* feature on the graphing calculator to find the point of intersection. The graphs intersect at (2, 3).

STEP 5 Check the solution

The x-value of the point of intersection, 2, is the solution of the equation.

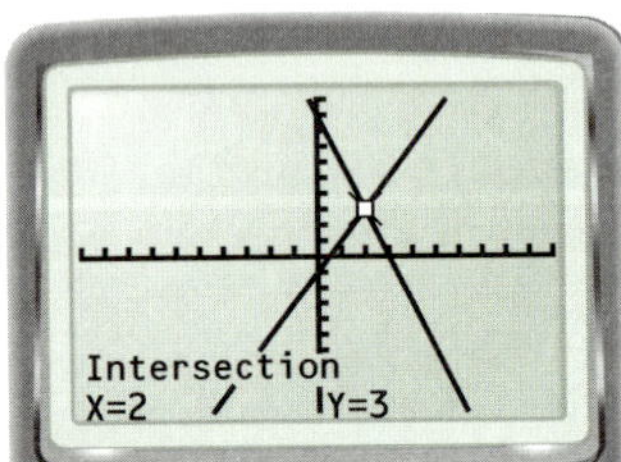

$$\text{Check:} \qquad 2t - 1 \overset{?}{=} -3t + 9$$
$$2(2) - 1 \overset{?}{=} -3(2) + 9$$
$$3 = 3 \checkmark$$

PRACTICE 2

Solve the equation using a graphing calculator.

7. $-5x + 2 = 4x - 7$

8. $7x - 4 = 9x - 8$

9. $-3x + 1 = -7x - 11$

10. $8x = 12x - 20$

11. $2x - 7 = 3x + 11$

12. $-x + 4 = x - 2$

13. DRAW CONCLUSIONS Describe the graphs when you solve an equation with a variable on one side by graphing each side of the equation. What is different about the graphs when the original equation has a variable on each side?

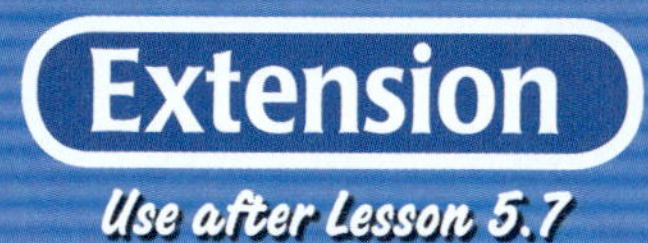

Assess the Fit of a Model

GOAL Assess the fit of a linear model by plotting and analyzing residuals.

Key Vocabulary
• residual

You have found lines of fit using estimation and using *linear regression.* Most lines of fit do not pass through every data point, so you can look at the *residuals* to assess whether the model is a good fit for the data.

RESIDUALS Given a set of data and a model, the difference between an actual value of the dependent variable y and the value predicted by the linear model $\hat{y}$ is called a **residual.** A *residual plot* is a scatter plot of points whose x-values are those from the data set and whose y-values are the corresponding residuals.

EXAMPLE 1 Calculate and interpret residuals

CRUISE SHIPS The table shows data for several cruise ships. Is the equation $y = 4x - 1500$ a good model for the data?

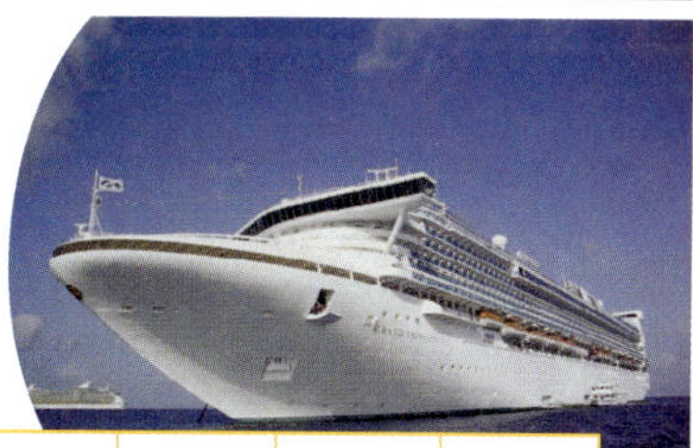

Length, x (ft)	644	720	754	781	866	915	965
Passenger capacity, y	1090	1266	1748	1440	1870	2435	1950

Solution

Make a table showing the passenger capacities predicted by the equation. Then calculate the residuals.

Length, x (ft)	644	720	754	781	866	915	965
Predicted capacity, $\hat{y}$	1076	1380	1516	1624	1964	2160	2360
Residuals, $y - \hat{y}$	14	−114	232	−184	−94	275	−410

Plot the residuals on a residual plot.

The equation $y = 4x - 1500$ models the data somewhat, but appears to predict capacity better for shorter lengths than it does for larger lengths.

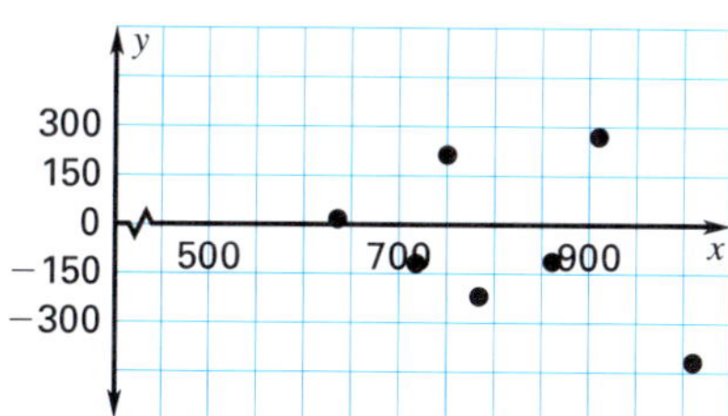

GOODNESS OF FIT If a line is a good fit for a set of data, the absolute values of the residuals are relatively small and more or less evenly distributed above and below the x-axis in a residual plot. Residuals that are mostly positive or mostly negative imply that the line is in the wrong place. Residuals that are steadily increasing suggest the data is not linear, while wildly scattered residuals suggest that the data might have relatively no correlation.

SAFETY The table shows stopping distances for cars based on the speed being traveled. Is the equation $y = 7x - 105$ a good model for the data?

Speed, x (mi/hr)	10	20	30	40	50	60	70	80	90	100
Stopping distance, y (ft)	27	63	109	164	229	303	387	481	584	696

Solution

Create a residual plot. The curve in the residuals suggests that a linear model may not be the best choice for this data, but for values of x between 20 and 80, this model appears to predict the actual value fairly well.

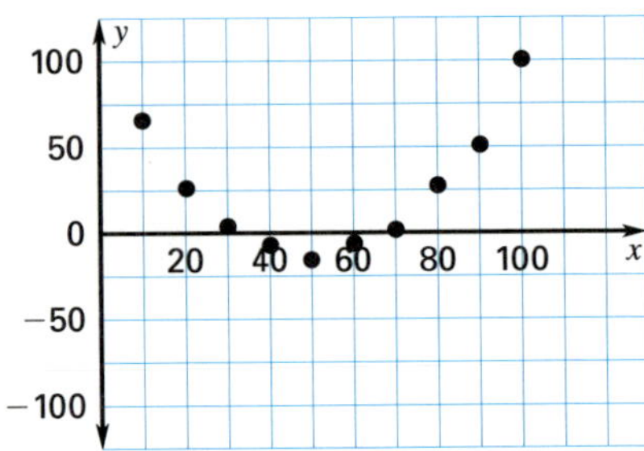

PRACTICE

For Exercises 1–4, the graph represents a residual plot for a data set and a linear model. Based on the residual plot, discuss the goodness of fit of the linear model.

1. 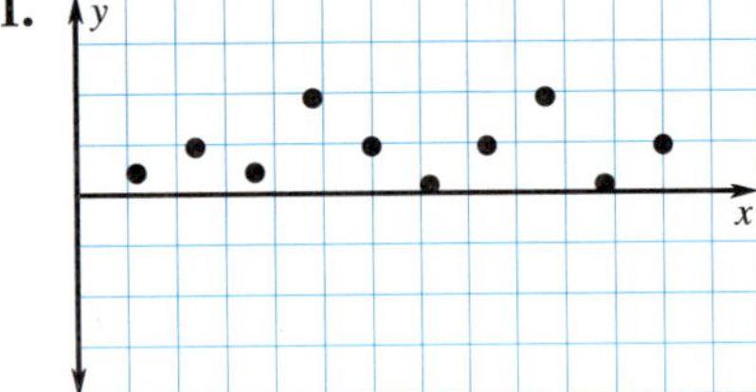

2. 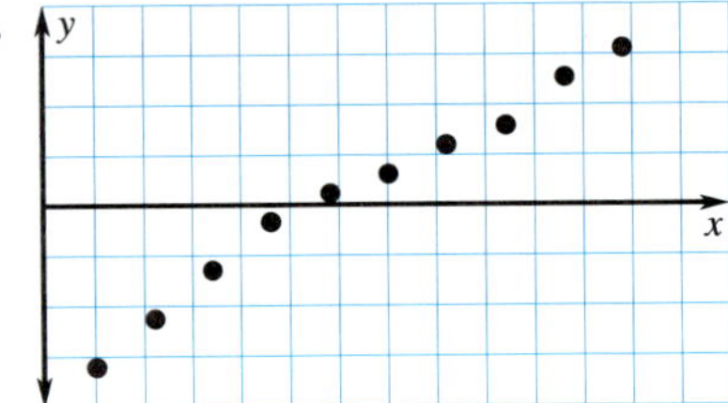

3. 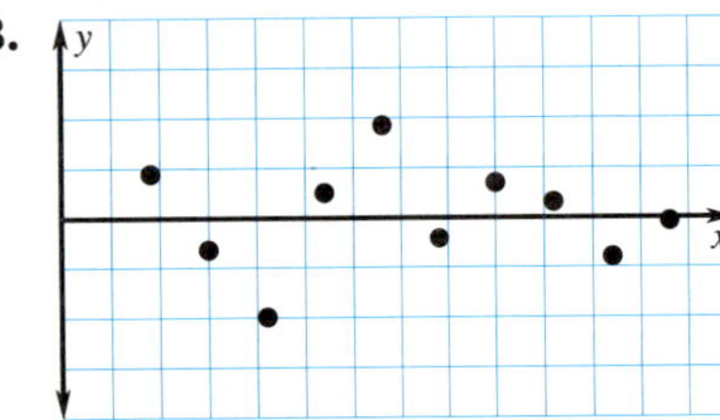

4. 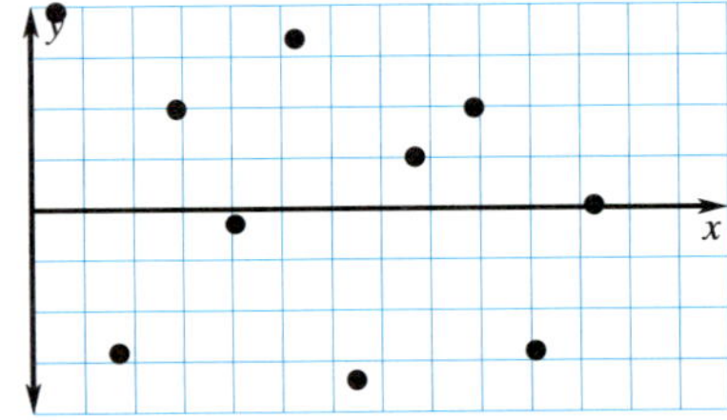

5. Create a residual plot for the data below using the model $y = 2x + 0.2$.

Time Walking, x (hr)	0	1	2	3	4	5
Distance Walked, y (mi)	0	2.1	4.3	6.1	8.6	10.1

Mastering *the* Standards

for Mathematical Practice

The topics described in the Standards for Mathematical Content will vary from year to year. However, the *way* in which you learn, study, and think about mathematics will not. The Standards for Mathematical Practice describe skills that you will use in all of your math courses.

Mathematical Practices

1. *Make sense of problems and persevere in solving them.*
2. *Reason abstractly and quantitatively.*
3. *Construct viable arguments and critique the reasoning of others.*
4. *Model with mathematics.*
5. *Use appropriate tools strategically.*
6. *Attend to precision.*
7. *Look for and make use of structure.*
8. *Look for and express regularity in repeated reasoning.*

5 Use appropriate tools strategically.

Mathematically proficient students consider the available tools when solving a... problem... [and] are... able to use technological tools to explore and deepen their understanding...

In your book

Problem Solving Workshops explore alternative methods as tools for problem solving. A variety of **Activities** use concrete and technological tools to explore mathematical concepts.

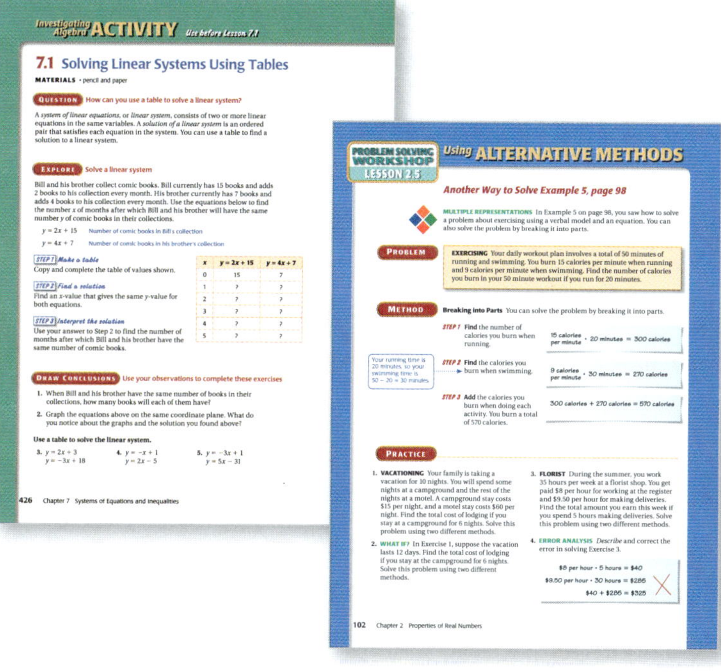

7.4 Multiply and Then Add Equations

QUESTION How can you see why elimination works as a method for solving linear systems?

You have used elimination to solve systems of linear equations, but you may think that it isn't obvious why this method works. You can do an algebraic proof by replacing the numbers in the system with variables, but this is complicated to do. In this activity, you will graph each equation that you get as you use elimination.

EXAMPLE 1 Solve the linear system using addition

Solve the linear system $\quad -2x + y = 1 \quad$ **Equation 1**
$\qquad\qquad\qquad\qquad\quad 2x + y = 5 \quad$ **Equation 2**

Solution

STEP 1 *Graph the System*

Solve both equations for y.

$$-2x + y = 1 \qquad 2x + y = 5$$
$$y = 1 + 2x \qquad y = 5 - 2x$$

Graph the two equations using a graphing calculator. Notice that the point of intersection of the graphs is the solution of the system.

The solution is $(1, 3)$.

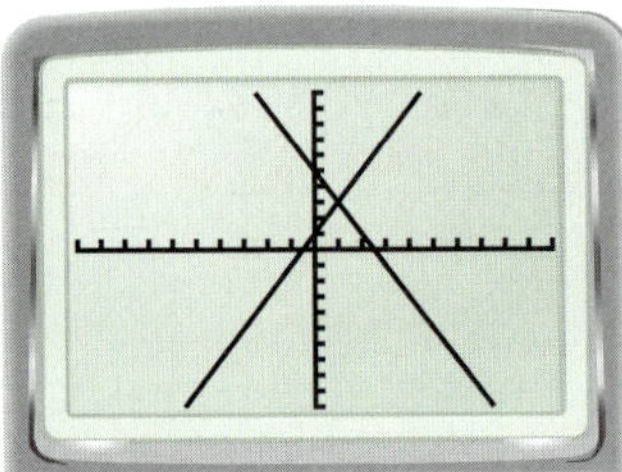

STEP 2 *Graph the sum of the equations*

Add the two equations as you would if you were solving the system algebraically. Graph the resulting equation.

$$\begin{array}{ll} -2x + y = 1 & \textbf{Equation 1} \\ \underline{2x + y = 5} & \textbf{Equation 2} \\ 2y = 6 & \textbf{Add.} \\ y = 3 & \textbf{Solve for y.} \end{array}$$

Now graph the equation $y = 3$ on the same graphing calculator screen with the two original equations.

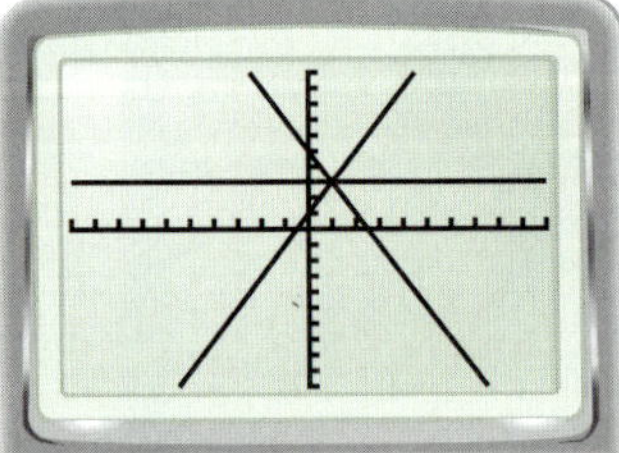

STEP 3 *Summarize the Results*

All three equations intersect at $(1, 3)$. So, $(1, 3)$ is the solution of the system.

PRACTICE 1

Solve the system using elimination. Graph each resulting equation.

1. $-x + y = 9$
$\ \ x + y = 1$

2. $6x - 7y = 4$
$\ \ x + 7y = 17$

3. $2x - 3y = 4$
$\ \ 8x + 3y = 1$

EXAMPLE 2 Solve a linear system using multiplication

Solve the linear system:

$$2x - y = 4 \qquad \text{Equation 1}$$
$$-3x + 2y = -7 \qquad \text{Equation 2}$$

STEP 1 Graph the System

Solve each equation for y.

$$2x - y = 4 \qquad\qquad -3x + 2y = -7$$

$$y = 2x - 4 \qquad\qquad y = \frac{3x - 7}{2}$$

Graph the two equations. The point of intersection of the graphs is the solution of the system.

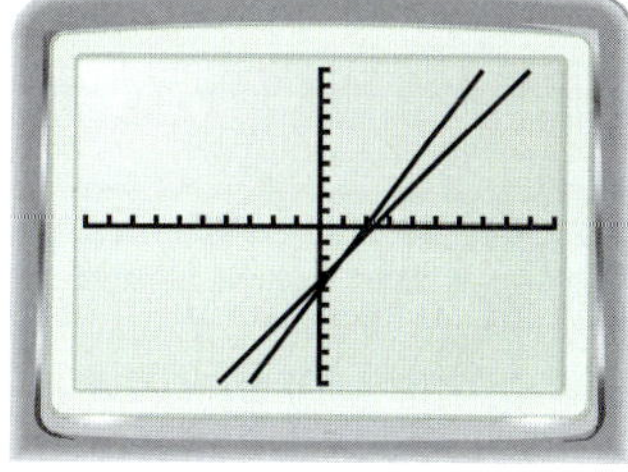

STEP 2 Use elimination to solve

Multiply each equation by a constant so that you can eliminate a variable x by adding.

$$2x - y = 4 \quad \times\,3 \quad\longrightarrow\quad 6x - 3y = 12 \qquad \textbf{Multiply Equation 1 by 3.}$$
$$-3x + 2y = -7 \quad \times\,2 \quad\longrightarrow\quad -6x + 4y = -14 \qquad \textbf{Multiply Equation 2 by 2.}$$
$$y = -2 \qquad \textbf{Add.}$$

STEP 3 Graph the resulting equations

Graph the equations $6x - 3y = 12$, $-6x + 4y = -14$, and $y = -2$ on the same graphing calculator screen with the two original equations.

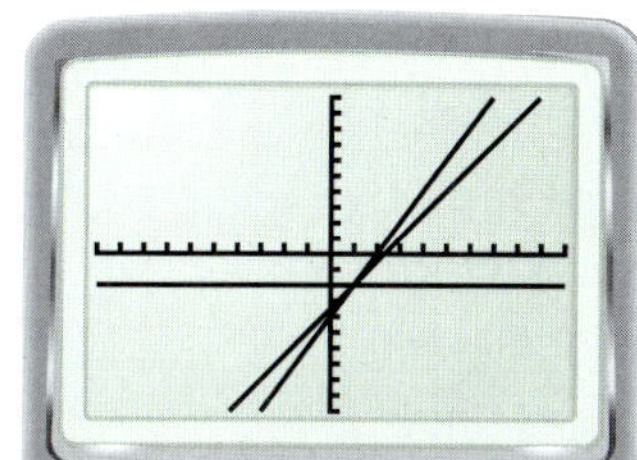

STEP 4 Summarize the Results

All of the equations intersect at $(1, -2)$. So, $(1, -2)$ is the solution of the system.

PRACTICE

Solve the system using elimination. Graph each resulting equation.

4. $x - y = -5$
$4x + 3y = 1$

5. $2x - 5y = 3$
$-x + 2y = -2$

6. $3x + 5y = 3$
$x - y = 9$

7. Solve the linear system using a graphing calculator. Now use a linear combination on the system to eliminate the variable x. Use a linear combination on the system to eliminate the variable y. What do you notice?

$$x - 2y = -6$$
$$2x + y = 8$$

DRAW CONCLUSIONS

8. Explain how you could use this method to check whether you have correctly solved a system of linear equations by graphing?

9. Suppose you are trying to solve a system of linear equations that has no solution.

  a. What happens when you use the elimination method?

  b. What does the graph of the system look like?

  c. Will the method of graphing the resulting equations as in Example 2 work with the system?

Mastering *the* Standards

for Mathematical Practice

The topics described in the Standards for Mathematical Content will vary from year to year. However, the *way* in which you learn, study, and think about mathematics will not. The Standards for Mathematical Practice describe skills that you will use in all of your math courses.

Mathematical Practices

1. *Make sense of problems and persevere in solving them.*
2. *Reason abstractly and quantitatively.*
3. *Construct viable arguments and critique the reasoning of others.*
4. *Model with mathematics.*
5. *Use appropriate tools strategically.*
6. *Attend to precision.*
7. *Look for and make use of structure.*
8. *Look for and express regularity in repeated reasoning.*

1 Make sense of problems and persevere in solving them.

Mathematically proficient students start by explaining to themselves the meaning of a problem... They analyze givens, constraints, relationships, and goals. They make conjectures about the form... of the solution and plan a solution pathway...

In your book

Verbal Models and the **Problem Solving Plan** help you translate the information in a problem into a model and then analyze your solution.

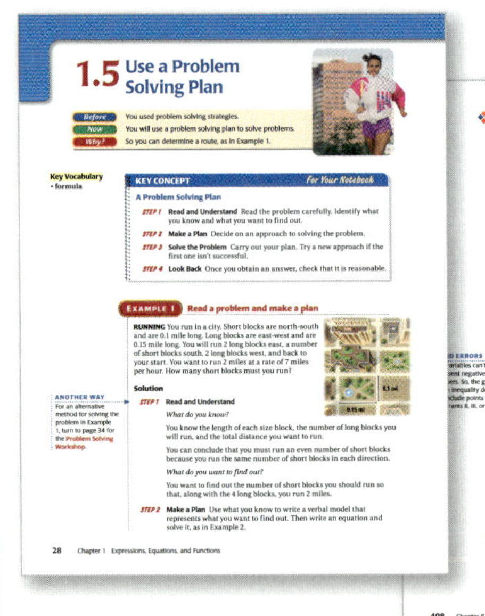

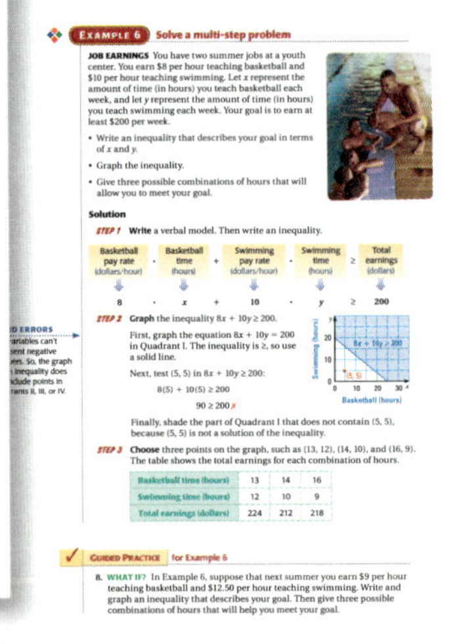

10.7A Solve Systems with Quadratic Equations

Before	You solved systems of linear equations.
Now	You will solve systems that include a quadratic equation.
Why?	So you can predict the path of a ball, as in Example 4.

You have solved systems of linear equations using the graph-and-check method and using the substitution method. You can use both of these techniques to solve a system of equations involving nonlinear equations, such as quadratic equations.

Recall that the substitution method consists of the following three steps.

STEP 1 **Solve** one of the equations for one of its variables.

STEP 2 **Substitute** the expression from Step 1 into the other equation and solve for the other variable.

STEP 3 **Substitute** the value from Step 2 into one of the original equations and solve.

EXAMPLE 1 **Use the substitution method**

Solve the system:

$$y = 3x + 2 \qquad \text{Equation 1}$$
$$y = 3x^2 + 6x + 2 \qquad \text{Equation 2}$$

Solution

STEP 1 **Solve** one of the equations for y. Equation 1 is already solved for y.

STEP 2 **Substitute** $3x + 2$ for y in Equation 2 and solve for x.

$$y = 3x^2 + 6x + 2 \qquad \text{Write original Equation 2.}$$
$$3x + 2 = 3x^2 + 6x + 2 \qquad \text{Substitute } 3x^2 + 2 \text{ for } y.$$
$$0 = 3x^2 + 3x \qquad \text{Subtract } 3x \text{ and 2 from each side.}$$
$$0 = 3x(x + 1) \qquad \text{Factor.}$$
$$3x = 0 \quad \text{or} \quad x + 1 = 0 \qquad \text{Zero-product property}$$
$$x = 0 \quad \text{or} \quad x = -1 \qquad \text{Solve for } x.$$

AVOID ERRORS
Be sure to set all linear factors equal to zero when applying the zero-product property.

STEP 3 **Substitute** both 0 and -1 for x in Equation 1 and solve for y.

$$y = 3x + 2 \qquad y = 3x + 2$$
$$y = 3(0) + 2 \qquad y = 3(-1) + 2$$
$$y = 2 \qquad \qquad y = -1$$

▶ The solutions are $(0, 2)$ and $(-1, -1)$.

POINTS OF INTERSECTION When you graph a system of equations, the graphs intersect at each solution of the system. For a system consisting of a linear equation and a quadratic equation the number of intersections, and therefore solutions, can be zero, one, or two.

Systems With One Linear Equation and One Quadratic Equation

There are three possibilities for the number of points of intersection.

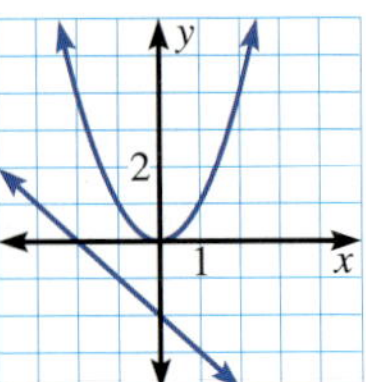

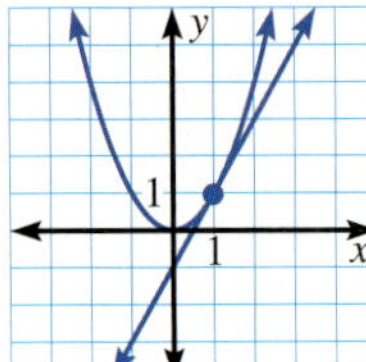

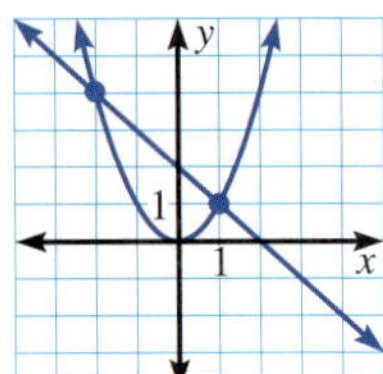

No Solution   **One Solution**   **Two Solutions**

EXAMPLE 2   **Use a graphing calculator to solve a system**

Solve the system: $y = 2x - 4$ **Equation 1**

$y = x^2 - 4x + 1$ **Equation 2**

Solution

STEP 1   Enter each equation into your graphing calculator.

Set $Y_1 = 2x - 4$ and $Y_2 = x^2 - 4x + 1$.

STEP 2   Graph the system. Set a good viewing window. For this system, a good window is $-10 \le x \le 10$ and $-10 \le y \le 10$.

STEP 3   Use the *Trace* function to find the coordinates of each point of intersection. The points of intersection are $(1, -2)$ and $(5, 6)$.

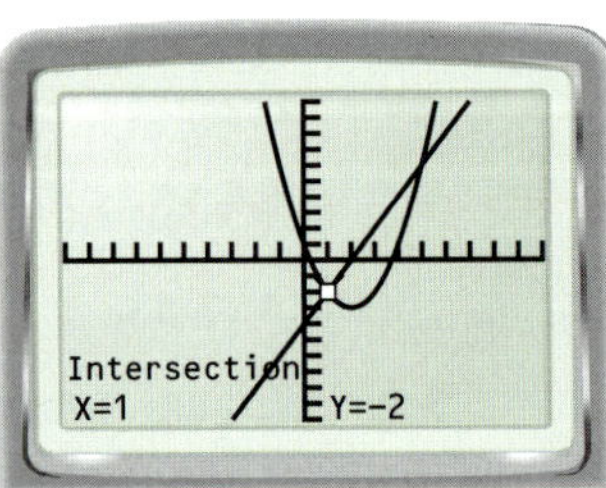

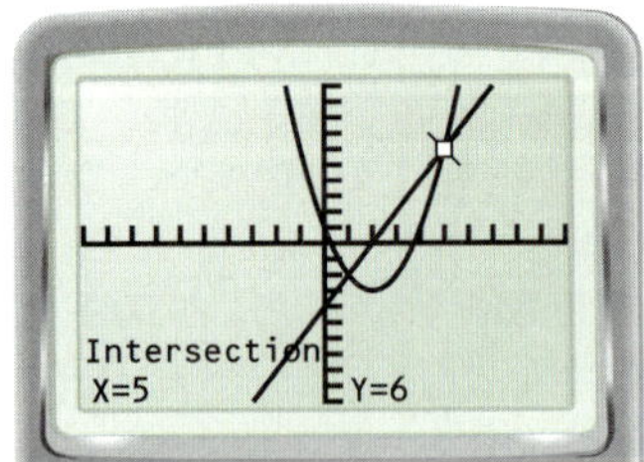

▶ The solutions are $(1, -2)$ and $(5, 6)$.

CHECK   Check the solutions. For example, check $(1, -2)$.

$$y = 2x - 4 \qquad y = x^2 - 4x + 1$$

$$-2 \stackrel{?}{=} 2(1) - 4 \qquad -2 \stackrel{?}{=} (1)^2 - 4(1) + 1$$

$$-2 = -2 \checkmark \qquad -2 = -2 \checkmark$$

Solve the system of equations first by using the substitution method and then by using a graphing calculator.

1. $y = x + 4$
$y = 2x^2 - 3x - 2$

2. $y = x + 1$
$y = -x^2 + 6x + 1$

3. $y = x^2 - 6x + 11$
$y = x + 1$

SOLVING EQUATIONS You can use a graph to solve an equation in one variable. Treat each side of the equation as a function. Then graph each function on the same coordinate plane. The x-value of any points of intersection will be the solutions of the equation

EXAMPLE 3 **Solve an equation using a system**

Solve the equation $-x^2 - 4x + 2 = -2x - 1$ using a system of equations. Check your solution(s).

Solution

STEP 1 Write a system of two equations by setting both the left and right sides of the given equation each equal to y.

$$-x^2 - 4x + 2 = -2x - 1$$

$$y = -x^2 - 4x + 2 \qquad \textbf{Equation 1}$$

$$y = -2x - 1 \qquad \textbf{Equation 2}$$

AVOID ERRORS
If you draw your graph on graph paper, be very neat so that you can accurately identify any points of intersection.

STEP 2 Graph Equation 1 and Equation 2 on the same coordinate plane or on a graphing calculator.

STEP 3 The x-value of each point of intersection is a solution of the original equation. The graphs intersect at $(-3, 5)$ and $(1, -3)$.

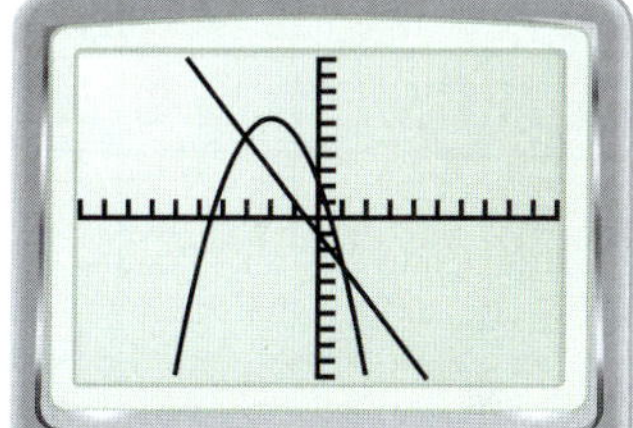

▶ The solutions of the equation are $x = -3$ and $x = 1$.

CHECK: Substitute each solution in the original equation.

$$-x^2 - 4x + 2 = -2x - 1 \qquad\qquad -x^2 - 4x + 2 = -2x - 1$$

$$-(-3)^2 - 4(-3) + 2 \stackrel{?}{=} -2(-3) - 1 \qquad -(1)^2 - 4(1) + 2 \stackrel{?}{=} -2(1) - 1$$

$$-9 + 12 + 2 \stackrel{?}{=} 6 - 1 \qquad\qquad -1 - 4 + 2 \stackrel{?}{=} -2 - 1$$

$$5 = 5 \checkmark \qquad\qquad\qquad -3 = -3 \checkmark$$

✓ **GUIDED PRACTICE** for Example 3

Solve the equation using a system of equations.

4. $x + 3 = 2x^2 + 3x - 1$

5. $x^2 + 7x + 4 = 2x + 4$

6. $8 = x^2 - 4x + 3$

7. $-x + 4 = 3^x$

BASEBALL During practice, you hit a baseball toward the gym, which is 240 feet away.

The path of the baseball after it is hit can be modeled by the equation:

$$y = -0.004x^2 + x + 3$$

The roof of the gym can be modeled by the equation:

$$y = \frac{2}{3}x - 120$$

for values of x greater than 240 feet and less than 320 feet.

The wall of the gym can be modeled by the equation:

$$x = 240$$

for values of y between 0 feet and 40 feet.

Does the baseball hit the roof of gym?

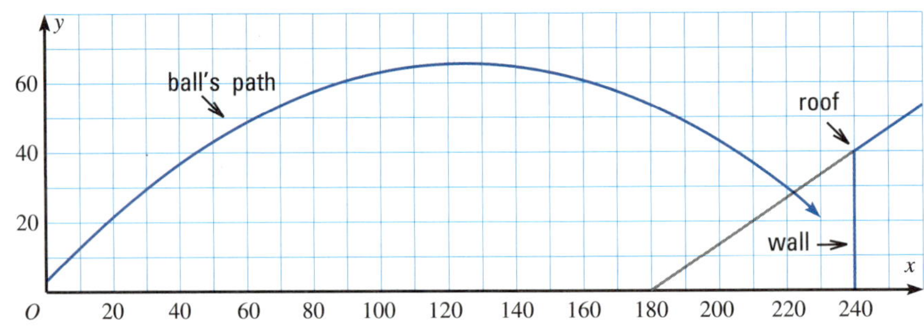

Solution

> *STEP 1* Write a system of two equations for the baseball and the roof.
>
> $$y = -0.004x^2 + x + 3 \qquad \textbf{Equation 1 (baseball)}$$
>
> $$y = \frac{2}{3}x - 120 \qquad \textbf{Equation 2 (roof)}$$

> *STEP 2* Graph both equations on the same coordinate plane.

> *STEP 3* The x-value where the graphs intersect is between 200 feet and 230 feet which is outside the domain of the equation for the roof.

▶ The baseball does not hit the roof.

 **GUIDED PRACTICE**   **for Example 4**

8. **WHAT IF?** In Example 4, does the baseball hit the gym wall? If it does, how far up the wall does it hit? If it does not, how far away from the gym wall does the ball land?

9. **WHAT IF?** In Example 4, if you hit the ball so that it followed a path that had a smaller number as the coefficient of x^2, would it be *more* or *less* likely to hit the gym? *Explain.*

© Tetra Images/Alamy

HOMEWORK KEY

◯ = **WORKED-OUT SOLUTIONS**
for Exs. 5, 15, 19, and 23

★ = **STANDARDIZED TEST PRACTICE**
Exs. 2, 11, 28, and 35

SKILL PRACTICE

1. **VOCABULARY** Describe how to use the substitution method to solve a system of linear equations.

2. ★ **WRITING** Describe the possible number of solutions for a system consisting of a linear equation and a quadratic equation.

EXAMPLE 1
on p. CC21
for Exs. 3–8

SUBSTITUTION METHOD Solve the system of equations using the substitution method.

3. $y = x^2 - x + 2$

   $y = x + 5$

4. $y = -x^2 + 4x - 2$

   $y = 4x - 6$

5. $y = x^2 - x$

   $y = -\dfrac{5}{2}x + 1$

6. $y = 2x^2 + x - 1$

   $y = -x - 3$

7. $y = 3x^2 - 6$

   $y = -3x$

8. $y = -2x^2 - 2x + 3$

   $y = \dfrac{7}{2}$

9. **ERROR ANALYSIS** Describe and correct the error in the solution steps shown.

$$y = 3x^2 - 6x + 4 \qquad \text{Equation 1}$$
$$y = 4 \qquad \text{Equation 2}$$
$$y = 3(4)^2 - 6(4) + 4 \qquad \text{Substitute.}$$
$$y = 3(16) - 24 + 4 = 28 \qquad \text{Simplify}$$

10. **COPY AND COMPLETE** When a system of equations includes a linear equation and a quadratic equation, there will (*always, sometimes, never*) be an infinite number of solutions.

11. ★ **MULTIPLE CHOICE** Which equation intersects the graph of $y = x^2 - 4x + 3$ twice?

    (A) $y = -1$

    (B) $x = 2$

    (C) $y + 1 = x$

    (D) $y + x = -1$

EXAMPLE 2
on p. CC22
for Exs. 12–17

GRAPHING CALCULATOR Use a graphing calculator to find the points of intersection, if any, of the graph of the system of equations.

12. $y = 3x^2 - 2x + 1$

    $y = x + 7$

13. $y = x^2 + 2x + 11$

    $y = -2x + 8$

14. $y = -2x^2 - 4x$

    $y = 2$

15. $y = \dfrac{1}{2}x^2 - 3x + 4$

    $y = x - 2$

16. $y = \dfrac{1}{3}x^2 + 2x - 3$

    $y = 2x$

17. $y = 4x^2 + 5x - 7$

    $y = -3x + 5$

EXAMPLE 3
on p. CC23
for Exs. 18–21

SOLVE THE EQUATION Solve the equation using a system. Check each answer.

18. $-5x + 5 = x^2 - 4x + 3$

19. $-6 = x^2 + 2x - 5$

20. $-3 = x^2 + 5x - 3$

21. $2x^2 + 4x = 2x + 4$

22. $y = -x^2 + 4$
  $y = 5$

23. $y = -1$
  $y = -2^x$

24. $y = x + 6$
  $y = 0.5^x$

25. $y = -x^2 + 2x$
  $y = -2x + 5$

26. $y = 3x - 1$
  $y = 2^x$

27. $y = -1.5x + 1$
  $y = 0.4^x$

28. ★ **WRITING** Describe the possible number of solutions for a system consisting of a quadratic equation and an exponential equation.

SOLVE THE EQUATION Solve the equation using a system.

29. $2^x + 1 = 2x + 1$

30. $4^x = -\dfrac{2}{3}x + 9$

31. $-2x + 11 = 2^x - 3$

32. $3^x - 5 = 6x - 8$

33. **CHALLENGE** Using a graphing calculator, find the points of intersection, if any, of the graphs of the equations $y = x^2 - 3x + 1$ and $y = x^2 - x - 1$. What are the solutions of the system?

PROBLEM SOLVING

EXAMPLES
1 AND 2
on p. CC21–22
for Exs. 34–36

34. **RECREATION** Marion and Reggie are driving boats on the same lake. Marion's chosen path can be modeled by the equation $y = -x^2 - 4x - 1$ and Reggie's path can be modeled by the equation $y = 2x + 8$. Do their paths cross each other? If so, what are the coordinates of the point(s) where the paths meet?

35. ★ **SHORT RESPONSE** Two dogs are running in a fenced dog park. One dog is following a path that can be modeled by the equation $y = 4$. Another dog is following a path that can be modeled by the equation $y = -x^2 + 3$. Will the dogs' paths cross? Explain your answer.

36. **ARCHITECTURE** The arch of the Sydney Harbor Bridge in Sydney, Australia, can be modeled by $y = -0.00211x^2 + 1.06x$ where x is the distance (in meters) from the left pylons and y is the height (in meters) of the arch above the water. The road can be modeled by the equation $y = 52$. To the nearest meter, how far from the left pylons are the two points where the road intersects the arch of the bridge?

⬭ = **WORKED-OUT SOLUTIONS**
  for Exs. 5, 15, 19, and 23

★ = **STANDARDIZED**
  TEST PRACTICE

EXAMPLES
3 AND 4

on p. CC22–24
for Exs. 37–39

37. **SAVINGS** Nancy and Miranda are looking at different ways to save money. Graph the two equations. Explain what happens when the graphs intersect. When will Miranda have more money saved than Nancy?

Nancy

I will save $15 each month.
My money will not earn interest.

A model for my savings is $y = 15x$.

x is the number of months
y is my total savings

Miranda

I will put $200 into an account that earns 2% annually. I will not save any more money.

If the interest is compounded monthly, $y = 200(1.02)^x$ models my savings.

x is months and y is my total savings.

38. **SPACE** Suppose an asteroid and a piece of space debris are traveling in the same plane in space. The asteroid follows a path that can be modeled locally by the equation $y = 2x^2 - 3x + 1$. The space debris follows a path that can be modeled locally by the equation $y = 8x - 13$.

   a. Will the paths of the two objects intersect? Is it possible for the two objects to collide? If so, what are the coordinates of the point where the paths intersect?

   b. What additional information would you need to decide whether the two objects will collide? *Explain*.

39. **MULTI-STEP PROBLEM** Keno asks Miguel if the graphs of all three of the equations shown below ever intersect in a single point.

$$y = 3x + 1 \qquad y = 2x^2 - 4x + 6 \qquad y = -2x + 6$$

   a. Find any points of intersection of the graphs of $y = 3x + 1$ and $y = 2x^2 - 4x + 6$.

   b. Find any points of intersection of the graphs of $y = 3x + 1$ and $y = -2x + 6$.

   c. Find any points of intersection of the graphs $y = 2x^2 - 4x + 6$ and $y = -2x + 6$.

   d. Do the three graphs ever intersect in a single point? If so, what are the coordinates of this point of intersection?

40. **CHALLENGE** Find the point(s) of intersection, if any, for the line with equation $y = -x - 1$ and the circle with equation $x^2 + y^2 = 41$.

MIXED REVIEW

PREVIEW

Prepare for
Lesson 10.8 in
Exs. 41–43.

Determine if the set of ordered pairs represents a function. *(Lesson 1.6)*

41. $(-2, 3), (3, 1), (-2, 5)$

42. $(4, 1), (-7, 1), (0.5, 1)$

43. $(3, -2), (3, 0.7), (3, 6)$

44. John's family is holding a garage sale and he needs to make a sign. His dad gives him a piece of cardboard to use that is $(2x - 5)$ inches long and $(3x + 2)$ inches wide. Write a quadratic expression in standard form that represents the area of the piece of cardboard. *(Lesson 9.2)*

10.8A Model Relationships

Before	You studied linear, exponential, and quadratic functions.
Now	You will compare representations of these functions.
Why	So you can model the height of water, as in Example 1.

Key Vocabulary
• Verbal Model
• Slope
• Vertex

Sometimes you will find it helpful to model a function with a graph even if you don't have enough information to write an equation to model the function.

Sketching a graph based on a description of a situation can help you understand the situation and identify key features of the model.

EXAMPLE 1 Sketch a graph of a real-world situation

FIRE-FIGHTING The water from one water cannon on a fire-fighting boat reaches a maximum height of 25 feet and travels a horizontal distance of about 140 feet.

   a. What type of function should you use to represent the path of the water? Sketch a graph of the path of the water.

   b. In the context of the given situation, what do the intercepts and maximum point represent?

Solution

   a. The path of the water can be modeled by a parabola. Let x represent the horizontal distance in feet and let y represent the vertical distance in feet.

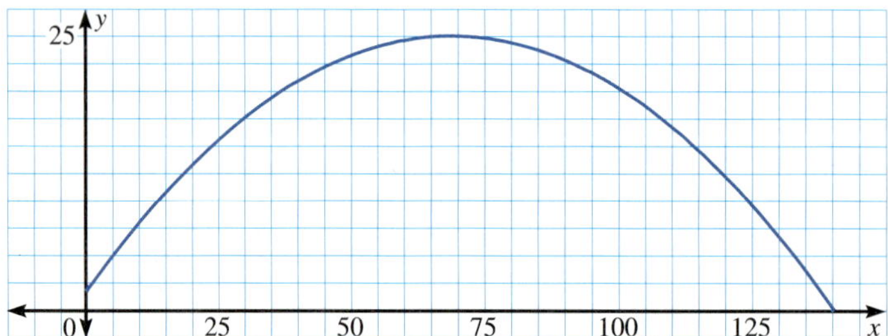

   b. Because the water cannon is on a boat, the graph has only one x-intercept where the water reaches the surface of the water or ground. The maximum point of the graph is where the water reaches its maximum height, about 70 feet from the boat.

✓ **GUIDED PRACTICE** for Example 1

   1. Using the graph in Example 1, describe the intervals in which the function is increasing and decreasing. Explain what the intervals mean in the given situation.

Decide which linear function is increasing at a greater rate.

- Linear Function 1 has an x-intercept of 4 and a y-intercept of -2.

- Linear Function 2 includes the points in the table below.

x	-2	-1	0	1	2	3
y	-11	-6	-1	4	9	14

Solution

AVOID ERRORS
In calculating the slope of a linear function, remember to divide the change in y by the change in x.

The slope of a linear equation indicates how rapidly a linear function is increasing or decreasing. The points $(4, 0)$ and $(0, -2)$ are on the graph of Linear Function 1, so its slope is $\dfrac{0 - (-2)}{4 - 0} = \dfrac{1}{2}$.

The table for Linear Function 2 shows that for each increase of 1 in the value of x there is an increase of 5 in the value of y, so its slope is $\dfrac{5}{1} = 5$.

▶ Linear Function 2 is increasing more rapidly.

Use the given information to decide which quadratic function has the lesser minimum value.

- Quadratic Function 1: The function whose equation is $y = 3x^2 - 12x + 1$.

- Quadratic Function 2: The function whose graph is shown at the right.

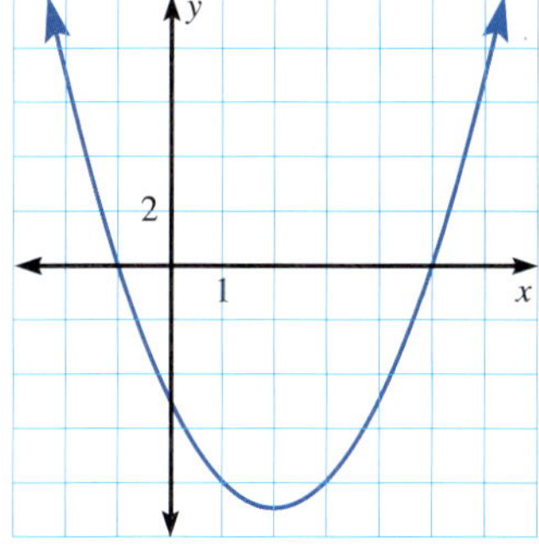

Solution

STUDY HELP
Review the lesson *Graph* $y = ax^2 + bx + c$ for information on finding the coordinates of the minimum value of a quadratic function.

The minimum value of Quadratic Function 1 is the y-value of the vertex of its parabola. The x-coordinate of the vertex is $-\left(\dfrac{b}{2a}\right) = -\dfrac{-12}{2(3)} = \dfrac{12}{6} = 2$. When $x = 2$, $y = 3(2)^2 - 12(2) + 1 = 12 - 24 + 1 = -11$. So the vertex is $(2, -11)$ and the minimum value is -11.

The minimum value of Quadratic Function 2 can be seen on the graph of the function; it is -9.

▶ Quadratic Function 1 has the lesser minimum value.

✓ **GUIDED PRACTICE** for Examples 2 and 3

2. COMPARE Compare the rates of change in the linear functions $y = 4x + 5$ and $y = 3 - 4x$.

3. WHAT IF? In Example 3, replace the equation for Quadratic Function 1 with $y = x^2 - 6x - 7$. Which function now has the lesser minimum value?

EXAMPLE 4   Choose a model for a real-world situation

BUSINESS The table shows the revenue generated by a company during each of the previous five years. Based on the change per unit interval, choose an appropriate type of function to model the situation.

Year	2008	2009	2010	2011	2012
Revenue ($)	50,000	51,500	53,045	54,636	56,275

Solution

The revenue is increasing each year by about 3%. Because the quantity grows by a constant percent rate per unit interval, you should use an exponential growth model for the situation.

EXAMPLE 5   Choose a model for a real-world situation

FURNITURE You are a furniture salesperson and earn $200 a week plus a 5% commission on the total value of all sales you make during the week.

a. Based on the given information, choose an appropriate type of function to model your potential weekly earnings as a function of sales.

b. Sketch a graph representing your potential earnings for any given week as a function of sales. Identify the function's intercept(s) and interpret the meaning of each intercept in the context of the given situation.

Solution

a. For every $100 of sales, your earnings increase by $5. Earnings are increasing by a constant rate. Use a linear function.

b. Let x represent the weekly sales and let y represent total earnings. The y-intercept is 200 and represents your weekly salary when you do not sell any furniture during that week. The function only makes sense for $x \geq 0$, so there is no x-intercept.

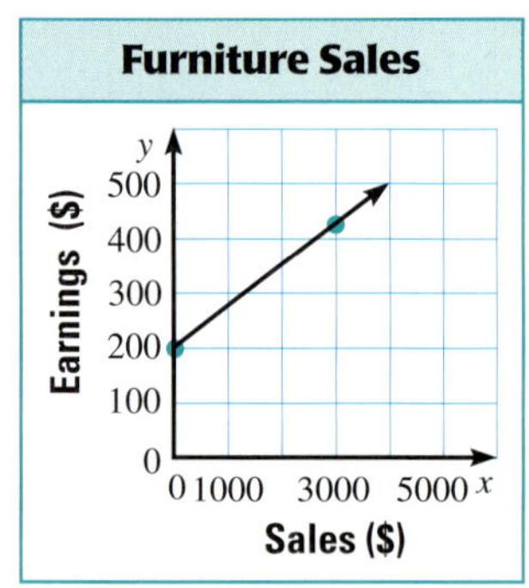

STUDY HELP
Remember that the graph of a real-world function does not necessarily have both an x-intercept and a y-intercept.

✓ **GUIDED PRACTICE**   for Examples 4 and 5

4. RUNNING The table shows the distance that Juan covered per hour in the first four hours of a triathlon. Based on the change per unit interval, choose an appropriate function to model the situation.

Hour	1	2	3	4
Miles	6	5.4	4.86	4.374

SKILL PRACTICE

1. **VOCABULARY** Copy and complete: A __?__ describes a real-world situation using words as labels and using math symbols to relate the words.

2. ★ **WRITING** Explain the relationship between the slope of a linear function and the concept of an increasing/decreasing linear function.

EXAMPLE 1
on p. CC28
for Exs. 3–5

3. **CHOOSE A MODEL** A hot air balloon has already risen 20 feet above the ground. At this point in time it begins to rise at a steady rate of 2 feet per second.

   a. What type of function would be a good model for this situation?

   b. Sketch a graph representing the balloon's altitude y in terms of the time x since it resumed its ascent.

   c. Identify the intervals on which the graph is increasing or decreasing and explain what these intervals mean in the context of the situation.

4. **CHOOSE A MODEL** During a weekend trip riding his motorcycle, Neil plans to average 55 miles per hour.

   a. What type of function would be a good model for this situation?

   b. Sketch a graph representing the distance he will travel y in terms of the number of hours x that he rides.

   c. Use the graph to identify the intercept(s) and interpret the meaning of each intercept in the context of the situation.

5. **CHOOSE A MODEL** A juggler throws a ball into the air. It reaches a maximum height of about 25 feet, and the juggler catches it again after 2.5 seconds.

   a. What type of function would be a good model for this situation?

   b. Sketch the graph of an equation that could model the height of the ball as a function of time.

   c. Identify the intervals on which the graph is increasing or decreasing and explain what these intervals mean in the context of the situation.

6. ★ **MULTIPLE CHOICE** Marvin is making a rectangular quilt. Suppose the width of the quilt is x meters and length of the quilt is $(3 - x)$ meters. Which type of function should you use to model the area y of the quilt in terms of its width?

   Ⓐ linear

   Ⓑ quadratic

   Ⓒ exponential growth

   Ⓓ exponential decay

© Wes Thompson/Corbis

7. A student uses a quadratic function to model a population that is increasing by 4% per year.

8. A student uses an exponential decay function to model the distance traveled over time of a car traveling at a steady speed of 50 miles per hour.

EXAMPLES
2 and 3
on p. CC29
for Exs. 9–10

9. **LINEAR FUNCTIONS** Use the given information to decide which linear function is decreasing more rapidly.

   • Linear Function 1 has a y-intercept of -3 and a slope of -1.

   • The table shows the coordinates of six points found on the line representing Linear Function 2.

x	-4	-2	0	2	4	6
y	8	4	0	-4	-8	-12

10. **QUADRATIC FUNCTIONS** Use the given information to decide which quadratic function has the greater maximum value.

    • Quadratic Function 1: The function whose equation is $y = -x^2 + 4x + 2$.

    • Quadratic Function 2: The function whose graph is shown at the right.

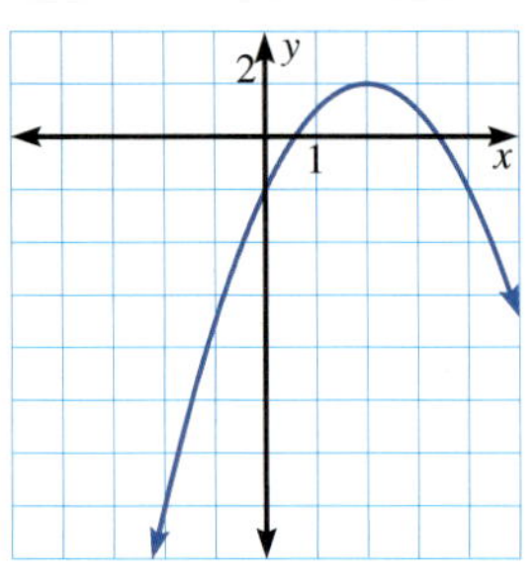

EXAMPLES
4 and 5
on p. CC30
for Exs. 11–12

11. ★ **MULTIPLE CHOICE** Decide which relationship grows by a constant percent rate per unit interval.

Ⓐ

Hours	1	2	3	4
Miles	5	10	15	20

Ⓑ

Year	1	2	3	4
Revenue ($)	2000	1500	1125	843.75

Ⓒ

Days	1	2	3	4
Windows Installed	2	4	8	16

Ⓓ

Minutes	1	2	3	4
Pancakes Made	27	9	3	1

12. **CHALLENGE** In 2010, the United States Census Bureau estimated that there were approximately 310 million people in the United States. By some estimates the population is growing by about 0.9% per year.

    a. Sketch a graph relating the population y at any time x. Let $x = 0$ represent the year 2010. What type of function will be a good model?

    b. Interpret the meaning of the x- and y-intercepts, if they exist, in terms of the context of this situation.

    c. Is the graph of the function increasing or decreasing? *Explain.*

○ = **WORKED-OUT SOLUTIONS**
for Exs. 2, 5, 11, and 15

★ = **STANDARDIZED**
TEST PRACTICE

**EXAMPLES
3 and 4**
on p. CC29
for Exs. 13–15

13. MUSIC Celia has already downloaded 14 songs to her cell phone. In the future she intends to download 2 songs per week. Her friend Connie has already downloaded 12 songs to her cell phone and she plans to download songs based on the table below. Which girl's playlist is growing faster?

Week	1	2	3	4
Total Number of Songs on Connie's Cell Phone	17	22	27	32

14. BASEBALL Tim threw a baseball in the air. Suppose the ball's height in feet can be modeled by the equation $y = -16x^2 + 40x + 5$. Matt threw the same baseball in the air. The graph models the height in feet of Matt's ball as a function of time. Which ball reached a greater height?

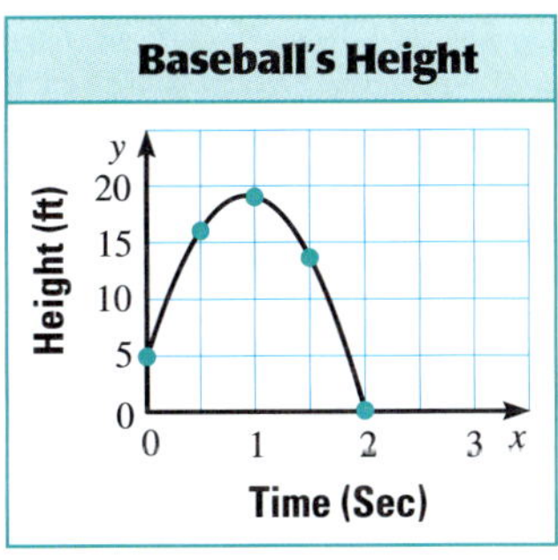

15. SCIENCE Tanya placed mold spores in a Petri dish. The table shows the number of spores in the dish at the end of each hour. Indicate whether the number of spores in the Petri dish represents *growth*, *decay*, or *neither*. Identify the growth or decay rate, if it exists, expressing it as a percent.

Hour	1	2	3	4
Number of Spores	16	24	36	54

16. CHICKENS You have 100 meters of fencing to build a chicken pen.

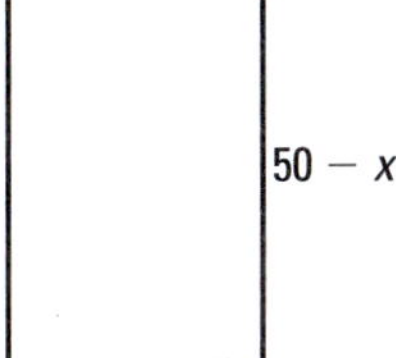

a. Use the diagram to help sketch a graph representing the area y of the pen in terms of the width x of the pen.

b. Use the graph to identify the intercept(s) and interpret the meaning of each intercept in the context of the situation.

17. ROWING The table shows the distance in miles that a rowing crew covered during each 15-minute interval in the first hour of practice. Based on the change per unit interval, choose an appropriate function to model the situation.

Minutes	15	30	45	60
Miles	2	1.6	1.28	1.024

18. **★ MULTIPLE CHOICE** Choose the situation in which one quantity changes by a constant amount per unit interval relative to a second quantity.

(A) Michael rented tables and chairs for a party. The cost for the rental was $10 for the first day. If he keeps them for more than one day the cost per day is double the preceding day.

(B) Alexi's stamp collection already contains 12 stamps. Each time he goes to the post office he will buy 2 stamps to add to his collection.

(C) Sue has an ant farm. The number of ants can be modeled by the equation $y = 100(1.05)^x$, where y is the number of ants on any given day and x is the number of days since she started the farm.

(D) Pam accidently dropped her watch from her tree house. The equation $y = -16x^2 + 37$ models the height of the watch as it is falling to the ground. The variable y represents the height of the watch and x represents the time in seconds since Pam dropped the watch.

19. **★ EXTENDED RESPONSE** Use the information to answer each question.

a. **Graphs** Using a single coordinate system, graph the functions $y = 2x$, $y = x^2$, and $y = 2^x$. Which function eventually has the greatest y-value for a given value of x?

b. **Tables** Complete a table similar to the one below for each of the three given functions. Which function eventually has the greatest y-value for a given value of x?

Linear Function: $y = 3x + 1$
Quadratic Function: $y = 3x^2 + 1$
Exponential Function: $y = 3^x + 1$

x	−1	0	2	4	6	8	10
y	?	?	?	?	?	?	?

c. **Challenge** Given any quantity that can be modeled by a linear function, any quantity that can be modeled by a quadratic function, and any quantity that can be modeled by an exponential growth function, can you predict which quantity will eventually exceed the other two? *Explain.*

20. **CHALLENGE** Evaluate the functions $y = ax + b$ and $y = a(b)^x$ for x equal to 0, 1, 2, 3, 4, and 5. In the case of the linear function, how does the value of the function change as the x-values increase 1 unit at a time? In the case of the exponential function how does the value of the function change as the x-values increase 1 unit at a time? Extend these findings to the families of linear and exponential functions.

MIXED REVIEW

PREVIEW
Prepare for Lesson 11.1 in Exs. 21–23

Evaluate the expression. *(Lesson 2.7)*

21. $\sqrt{49}$

22. $-\sqrt{81}$

23. $\pm\sqrt{200}$

Solve the equation. Round your solutions to the nearest hundredth, if necessary. *(Lesson 10.5)*

24. $32 = x^2 + 7$

25. $2q^2 - 5 = 62$

26. $3x^2 - 25 = 38$

○ = **WORKED-OUT SOLUTIONS** for Exs. 2, 5, 11, and 15   ★ = **STANDARDIZED TEST PRACTICE**

10.8A Average Rate of Change

QUESTION What is the average rate of change between two points?

The *average rate of change* is useful for some real-world situations, like finding the average growth rate of a tree over a 20-year period. You can use the slope formula to find the average rate of change between two points on the graph of a non-linear function.

EXAMPLE Find an average rate of change

Find the average rate of change between points on the graph of $y = 2x^2 - 3x - 1$. How does the choice of the points impact the average rate of change?

STEP 1 *Graph the function*

Graph the function on a graphing calculator. Then use the *Trace* feature to identify the coordinates of points on the graph. Record four pairs of points in a table like the one shown.

STEP 2 *Calculate average rate of change*

Calculate the average rate of change between the points in each pair by calculating the slope of the line through the two points. Record the results. Add a column for the absolute values of the average rates of change.

Points	Average Rate of Change	Absolute Value of the Average Rate of Change
(2, 1), (3, 8)	7	7
(−0.1, −0.68) (0, −1)	−0.32	0.32

Depending on the pair of points chosen for an interval, notice that the average rate of change can be positive or negative, and either very large or very small.

DRAW CONCLUSIONS

In Exercises 1–4, repeat Steps 1 and 2 for the given function.

1. $y = 2x - 3$ **2.** $y = -4x^2 + 2x - 1$ **3.** $y = 10 \cdot 2^x$ **4.** $y = 2\left(\dfrac{1}{3}\right)^x$

5. Graph the functions given in the table below. Estimate the average rate of change for each graph. Copy and complete the table. Generalize the results.

Function	$\dfrac{f(10) - f(0)}{10 - 0}$	$\dfrac{f(100) - f(10)}{100 - 10}$	$\dfrac{f(1000) - f(100)}{1000 - 100}$	$\dfrac{f(10{,}000) - f(1000)}{10{,}000 - 1000}$
$y = x + 1$	1	1	?	?
$y = x^2 + 1$	10	110	?	?
$y = 2^x$	102.3	?	?	?

13.5 Investigating Samples

MATERIALS · red beans, pinto beans, container

QUESTION How well do different samples represent a situation?

EXPLORE Select a sample

STEP 1 *Create the population* Drop 80 pinto beans into a container. Place 20 red beans directly on top of the pinto beans. Then out of 100 beans in the jar, twenty percent of the beans are red beans.

STEP 2 *Take a sample* Without stirring, reach in and pull a handful of beans out of the jar. Count the number of red beans and the total number of beans in your handful. Record your results in a table like the one below. Return the beans to the jar.

STEP 3 *Take a second sample* Stir the jar thoroughly. Pull a handful of beans out of the jar. Record your results of this sample in your table. Return the beans to the jar.

STEP 4 *Take a third sample* Stir the jar thoroughly. Pull a handful of beans out of the jar. Add your results to your table.

Sample	Number of red beans, b	Total number of beans, T	Percent that is red (b/T)
one handful, not stirred	?	?	?
one handful, stirred	?	?	?
two handfuls, stirred	?	?	?

DRAW CONCLUSIONS Use your observations to complete these exercises

1. Compare the first two samples.

   a. How does stirring affect the results?

   b. Which sample seems to be more representative of the beans in the jar? Why do you think this occurred?

   c. How could you accomplish the same effect as stirring the beans when choosing a real-world sample for a survey or study?

2. Compare the last two samples. Which of these samples seems to be more representative of the beans in the jar? *Explain.*

3. You would like to perform a fourth trial. Which of the samples below do you think would produce the most representative sample? *Explain* your reasoning.

   A 20 beans poured out, unstirred   **B** two handfuls, stirred

   C three handfuls, stirred   **D** three handfuls, unstirred

13.6A Analyze Data

Before	You found measures of central tendency.
Now	You will find relative frequencies in a two-way frequency table.
Why?	So you can use data about dogs in a store in Exercise 3 on p. CC39.

Key Vocabulary
• **marginal frequency**
• **joint frequency**

A two-way frequency table shows the number of items in various categories. Every element in the sample must fit into one of the categories and there must be no overlap between categories.

KEY CONCEPT
For Your Notebook

Two-way frequency table

A two-way frequency table divides the data into categories across the top and down the side.

	Apples	Oranges	Total
Boys	15	18	33
Girls	21	16	37
Total	36	34	70

The body of the table gives the **joint frequencies**.

The row and column totals give the **marginal frequencies**.

EXAMPLE 1 Read information from a two-way frequency table

The table shows the results of students naming their favorite subject.

	Math	Science	English	Total
Miss Bailey's homeroom	8	6	5	19
Mr. Cole's homeroom	4	7	9	20
Total	12	13	14	39

a. How many students in Miss Bailey's homeroom prefer math?

b. How many students from both homerooms prefer science?

Solution

a. The cell in the row for Miss Bailey's homeroom and in the column for Math contains 8, so 8 students in her homeroom prefer math.

b. The cell in the total row and in the column for Science contains 13, so 13 students prefer Science.

Make a two-way frequency table for the following data.

There are 175 freshmen taking a foreign language. Of these, 88 take Spanish, 46 take French, and the rest take German. No one takes more than one language. There are 42 boys taking Spanish, 31 girls taking French, and a total of 89 girls taking a language.

Solution

The categories are Spanish, French, German, boys, and girls. Fill in the given information. Then look for ways to calculate the missing values.

For example, the number of girls taking Spanish is $88 - 42 = 46$. The number of boys taking a foreign language is $175 - 89 = 86$. The total number of students taking German is $175 - (88 + 46)$.

AVOID ERRORS
Be sure to enter the given information in the correct cells of the table.

	Spanish	French	German	Total
Boys	42	15	29	86
Girls	46	31	12	89
Total	88	46	41	175

✓ **GUIDED PRACTICE**   **for Examples 1 and 2**

1. Using the table in Example 1, tell whether more students in Mr. Cole's homeroom prefer science or English.

2. There are 152 students who play golf, basketball, or soccer. No one plays more than one of these sports. There are 22 who play golf, 50 who play basketball, and the rest play soccer. There are 10 boys who play golf, 26 girls who play basketball, and a total of 80 boys who play one of these sports. Make a two-way frequency table for the data.

EXAMPLE 3   **Analyze a situation in a two-way table**

The table shows where students at a university live.

	Live on Campus	Live off Campus	Total
Men	3216	4010	7226
Women	3824	3758	7582
Total	7040	7768	14,808

a. Do more students live on campus or off campus?

b. Is it also true that more women live off campus than on campus?

Solution

a. Look at the marginal frequencies in the Total row. More students live off campus.

b. No. Even though the marginal frequencies show that more students live off campus, looking at just the row for women, you can see that more women live on campus than off campus.

13.6A EXERCISES

SKILL PRACTICE

1. **VOCABULARY** copy and complete: The body of a two-way frequency table gives the __?__ of the categories involved.

2. ★ **WRITING** Explain how you find the marginal frequency of a category in a two-way frequency table. Give an example.

EXAMPLE 1
on p. CC37
for Exs. 3–5

READING A TWO-WAY TABLE Answer the questions based on the table showing the number of different kinds of puppies at a pet store.

	Labradors	Poodles	Yorkies	Total
Males	7	5	3	15
Females	4	8	6	18
Total	11	13	9	33

3. How many male poodles does the pet store have?

4. How many female puppies does the pet store have?

5. How many more labradors than yorkies does the pet store have?

EXAMPLE 2
on p. CC38
for Exs. 6–7

6. **COPY AND COMPLETE** Copy and complete the two-way table showing data about cars sold.

	2 door	4 door	Total
6 cylinder	586	?	?
8 cylinder	?	840	?
Total	?	1564	2465

7. **MAKING A TWO-WAY TABLE** You surveyed 82 students in your grade and found that twenty-three have 2 brothers and twenty-eight have 1 brother. Nine students are only children, ten have only 1 sister, seven have only 1 brother, six have 2 sisters and 1 brother, twenty-two have 2 sisters, twenty-seven have no sisters, and eight have 1 sister and 2 brothers. Make a two-way frequency table of the given information.

8. ★ **MULTIPLE CHOICE** Use this two-way table to find how many 4 bedroom houses with 3 baths are for sale.

	3 Bedroom	4 Bedroom	Total
1 Bath	10	1	11
2 Bath	68	47	115
3 Bath	31	75	106
Total	109	122	232

(A) 31　　　(B) 47　　　(C) 68　　　(D) 75

ANALYZING A TWO-WAY TABLE The table shows the number of votes each student received from the various classes in the Student Government President Election.

	Freshmen	Sophomores	Juniors	Seniors	Total
Matt	92	86	110	71	359
Olivia	77	99	82	68	326
Katy	115	94	90	149	448
Total	284	279	282	288	1133

9. If Matt received the most votes from the students in his class, what year student is Matt?

10. Did any candidate have the most votes from more than one class? If so, who and which classes? *Explain.*

11. Which student won the election?

12. **CHALLENGE** Create a two-way table from the given information. Water and iced tea come in 12-ounce and 16-ounce bottles. The number of 16-ounce bottles is one less than the number of 12-ounce bottles. There are 11 more bottles of iced tea than water. There are 16 bottles of water and the number of 12-ounce bottles of water is 2 less than twice the number of 16-ounce bottles of water.

PROBLEM SOLVING

In Exercises 13–15, use the given two-way table showing sandwiches sold at a deli to answer the questions.

	Ham	Chicken	Salami	Total
White bread	65	41	37	143
Wheat bread	97	75	62	234
Total	162	116	99	377

13. **SANDWICHES** How many more ham sandwiches on wheat bread were sold than chicken sandwiches on white bread?

14. **PREDICT** If you choose one sandwich at random would it be more likely to be chicken on wheat bread or ham on white bread? *Explain.*

15. ★ **SHORT RESPONSE** If you know that a customer is going to order a sandwich on wheat bread, what is the most likely type of sandwich that customer will order? *Explain.*

16. **MUSIC** There are 33 students in choir and 74 in band. No one is in both. Twenty-three of these students are less than 5 feet tall and 24 are more than 6 feet tall. Six choir members are less than 5 feet tall while twenty-two choir members are between 5 and 6 feet tall.

 a. How many students in the choir are more than 6 feet tall?

 b. How many students in the band are between 5 and 6 feet tall?

 c. If you choose a student at random from the choir and from the band, which student is more likely to be between 5 and 6 feet tall? *Explain.*

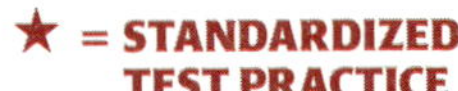

★ = STANDARDIZED
TEST PRACTICE

17. **VEGETABLES** A gardener planted two tomato and green pepper plants in each of two types of soil to test fertilizers. The table shows the number of tomatoes and green peppers harvested from each set of plants. Which type of soil seems better for each vegetable?

	Tomatoes	Green Peppers	Total
Fertilizer- fortified soil	56	37	93
Soil fertilized every 2 weeks	65	19	84
Total	121	56	177

a. Does one treatment appear to better for tomatoes?

b. Does one treatment appear to better for green peppers?

c. Looking at just the totals, which treatment appears to be better? Is this the best choice for both types of plants? *Explain.*

18. ★ **EXTENDED RESPONSE** Sangee, Tom, and Maleho have classical and rock CDs. They have a total of 141 CDs, of which 47 are classical. Sangee has 19 rock CDs and 26 classical CDs, Tom has 38 rock CDs, and Maleho has 49 CDs.

a. Model Make a two-way table to display this data.

b. Calculate If Sangee bought a classical CD, how would his classical CD total compare to Maleho's rock CD total?

c. Analyze If a CD is chosen at random from those owned by these three boys, would it be more likely to be classical or rock?

19. **CHALLENGE** There were 1809 tickets sold to a play, of which 800 were for the main floor. These tickets consisted of $2x + y$ adult tickets on the main floor, $x - 40$ child tickets on the main floor, $x + 2y$ adult tickets in the balcony, and $3x - y - 80$ child tickets in the balcony.

a. Find the values of x and y.

b. Find the number of adult balcony tickets sold.

c. Find the number of child main floor tickets sold.

MIXED REVIEW

PREVIEW

Prepare for Lesson 13.7 in Ex. 20

Factor the polynomial. *(Lesson 9.5)*

20. $4x^2 - 8x$ **21.** $a^2 + 5a + 4$ **22.** $h^2 - h - 72$

Factor the polynomial. *(Lesson 9.6)*

23. $2x^2 + x - 3$ **24.** $36x^2 - 60x + 25$ **25.** $9y^2 - 3y - 2$

26. The value of Michael's car decreases by about 10% per year. If you write a model for the value of his car over time, should you use a *linear function*, a *quadratic function*, or an *exponential function*? *(Lesson 10.8A)*

27. Over the last several years, Maria's collection of lunchboxes has increased by about 5 lunchboxes a year. If you write a model to predict the size of her collection in 3 years, should you use a *linear function*, a *quadratic function*, or an *exponential function*? *(Lesson 10.8A)*

13.7 Investigate Dot Plots

MATERIALS · ruler, graph paper

QUESTION How do you represent data in a dot plot?

Data can be represented by dots in a display called a dot plot. A dot plot shows the frequency of data and how the data are distributed.

EXPLORE Draw a dot plot

STEP 1 *Collect data*

Look up the low temperature for a city in the northern United States for each day in January of last year.

STEP 2 *Make a dot plot*

Use graph paper to draw a horizontal axis. Label it Temperatures and number it using a reasonable scale. Place a dot above the appropriate temperature to represent the low temperature for each day in January. For example, put a dot over the temperature 4 to indicate that the low temperature on one day was 4°F. The sample graph shows that it was 4°F on two days and −3°F on one day.

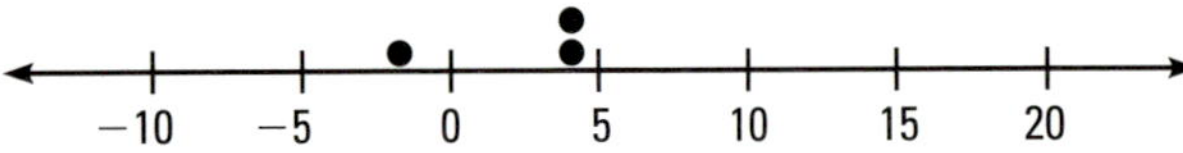

DRAW CONCLUSIONS Use your observations to complete these exercises

1. Examine your dot plot. What is the range of the data values?

2. Are the data tightly clustered or spread apart?

3. Is there a value that occurs more often than the others? If so, what does this mean in the context of the data?

4. If you were to add the temperature for February 1st to your dot plot, what would you expect it to be? Explain your reasoning. What types of values would be surprising? Why?

5. How would your dot plot change if you collected temperatures from a summer month rather than from January?

6. Compare the data in the dot plots.

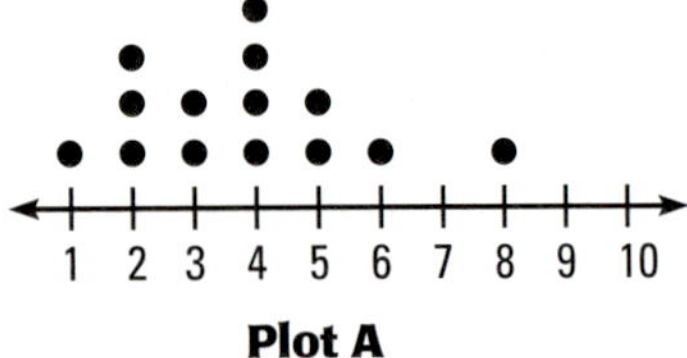

Plot A

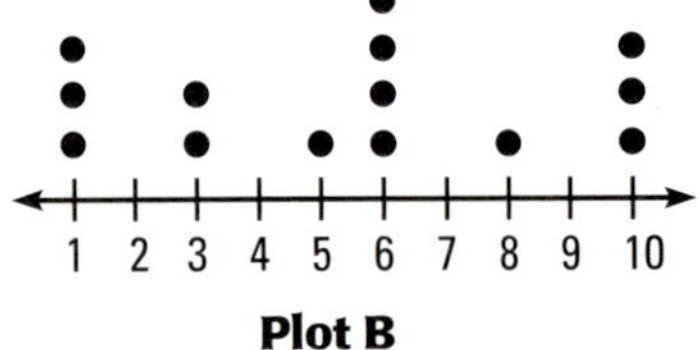

Plot B

Mastering the **Standards**

for Mathematical Practice

The topics described in the Standards for Mathematical Content will vary from year to year. However, the *way* in which you learn, study, and think about mathematics will not. The Standards for Mathematical Practice describe skills that you will use in all of your math courses.

Mathematical Practices

1. *Make sense of problems and persevere in solving them.*
2. *Reason abstractly and quantitatively.*
3. *Construct viable arguments and critique the reasoning of others.*
4. Model with mathematics.
5. *Use appropriate tools strategically.*
6. *Attend to precision.*
7. *Look for and make use of structure.*
8. *Look for and express regularity in repeated reasoning.*

4 Model with mathematics.

Mathematically proficient students can apply... mathematics... to... problems... in everyday life, society, and the workplace...

In your book

Application exercises and **Mixed Reviews of Problem Solving** apply mathematics to other disciplines and in real-world scenarios.

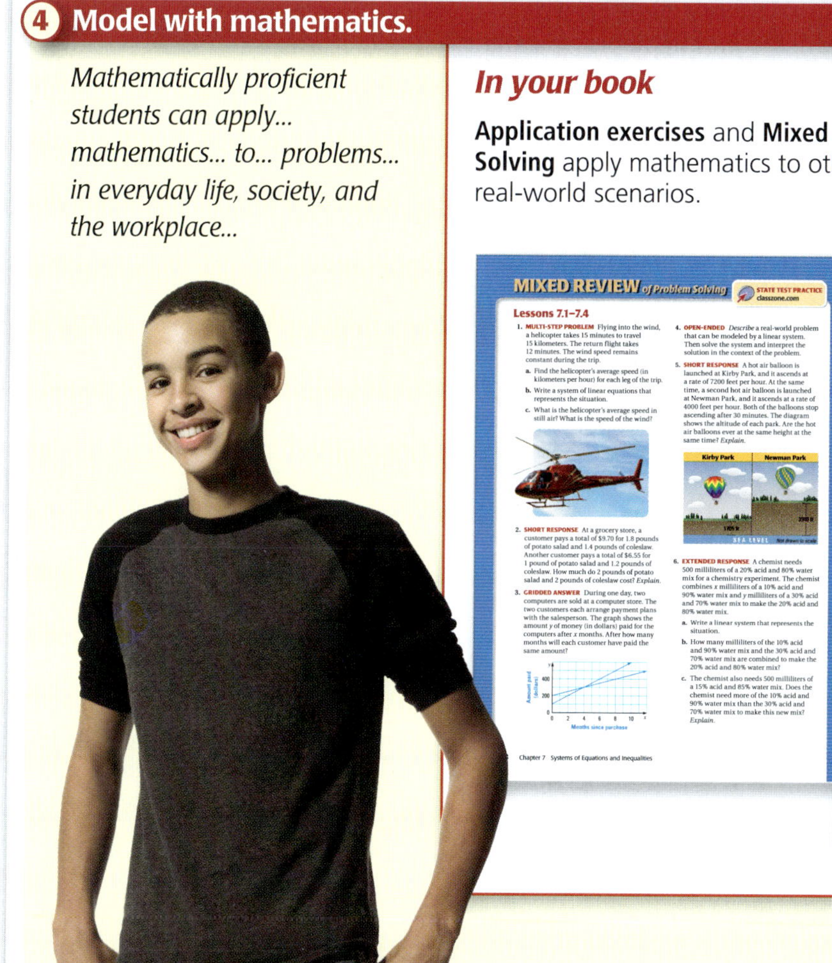

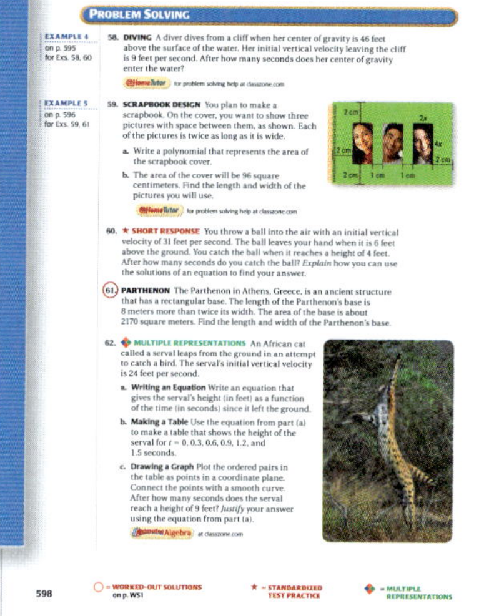

Analyze Data Distribution

GOAL Choose an appropriate display, measure of central tendency, and measure of spread based on the shape of a data distribution.

When you are presenting a set of data, you should consider the distribution of the data before deciding what type of measure of central tendency and graph to use for the data.

DATA THAT ARE CLOSELY GROUPED Use a histogram to display the data. Use the mean as a measure of central tendency. Use standard deviation as a measure of the spread.

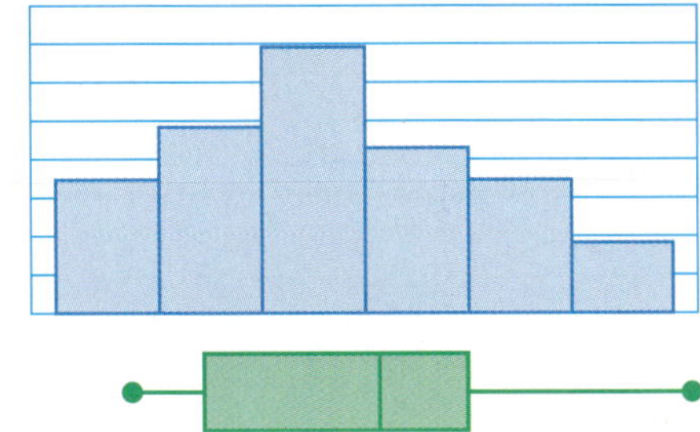

DATA VALUES THAT ARE SPREAD OUT Use a box-and-whisker plot to display the data. Use the median as a measure of central tendency. Use the interquartile range as a measure of the spread.

EXAMPLE 1 **Choose a display for data**

A used car dealer has 21 cars for sale at the prices shown in the table. Choose an appropriate display, measure of central tendency, and measure of spread for this data set.

$2150	$2800	$3500	$5100	$6050	$7100	$7250
$8000	$8850	$9100	$9225	$9900	$10,200	$10,800
$11,750	$12,200	$12,640	$13,020	$14,700	$15,500	$16,400

Solution

The data are close together with no outliers. Use a histogram. The center of the data can be represented by the mean, which is $9,345. The spread can be represented by the standard deviation, which is about $3946.

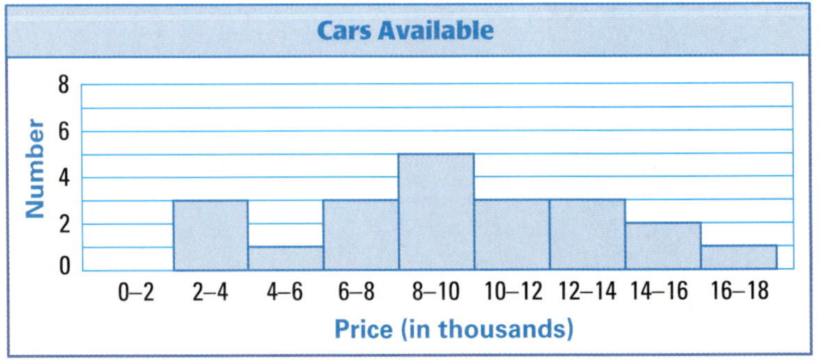

Another used car dealer has 24 cars for sale at the prices shown in the table. Choose an appropriate display, measure of central tendency, and measure of spread for this data set.

$3,800	$5,100	$7,100	$7,250	$8,850	$9,225	$9,900	$10,200
$10,500	$10,800	$11,400	$11,750	$12,200	$12,350	$12,640	$13,020
$13,890	$14,700	$15,500	$15,990	$17,000	$17,800	$22,900	$38,775

Solution

The data value $38,775 appears to be an outlier. Use a box-and-whisker plot to display the data. The outlier will affect the mean and standard deviation, so they do not represent the data well. The median is $11,975. The interquartile range is $5537.50.

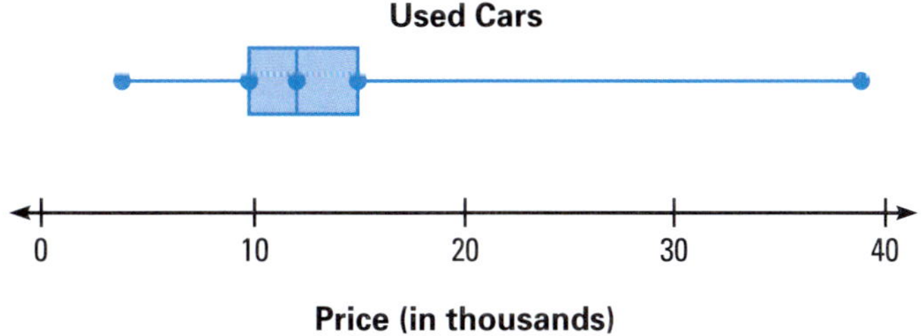

EXERCISES

For Exercises 1–6, choose an appropriate display, measure of central tendency, and measure of spread for the data set. Explain your reasoning.

1. **QUIZ SCORES** The scores on the first quiz in Mr. Stuart's math class were 6, 9, 10, 12, 12, 13, 14, 14, 15, 15, 15, 16, 16, 17, 17, 17, 17, 18, 18, 18, 19, 19, 19, 20, and 20.

2. **FOOTBALL** The points scored by twenty of the top 25 college football teams on Saturday, September 25, 2010 were 24, 73, 37, 42, 17, 31, 70, 35, 10, 20, 37, 65, 22, 31, 20, 24, 12, 27, 14, and 34.

3. **RUNNING** The time (in minutes) it took twenty freshmen to run the mile in physical education class were 7, 7.5, 8, 8, 8.2, 8.4, 8.5, 9, 9, 9, 9.6, 9.8, 10, 10.5, 10.5, 10.8, 11.2, 11.5, 11.7, and 12 minutes.

4. **HOMEWORK** The numbers of hours that twenty-five students spent doing homework last week were 1, 8, 8, 8.5, 9, 9.5, 9.5, 10, 10, 10, 10, 10, 10.5, 10.5, 10.5, 11, 11, 11, 11, 11.5, 11.5, 12, 12, 12, and 12.

5. **COOKIES** The numbers of cookies in 20 boxes at a bake sale are 16, 16, 18, 18, 20, 20, 24, 24, 24, 24, 26, 28, 28, 30, 30, 30, 30, 36, 36, and 36.

6. **BASEBALL** The attendance at a professional baseball team's home games during September are shown in the table.

39,555	31,424	40,788	31,647	31,596	33,623
36,364	37,285	34,481	36,553	39,316	38,057